The Exodus

And the Wanderings in the Wilderness

By Alfred Edersheim

PANTIANOS
CLASSICS

Published by Pantianos Classics

ISBN-13: 978-1-78987-653-6

First published in 1875

The Siniatic Peninsula

(*From the Ordnance Survey.*)

Contents

Preface

The period covered by the central books of the Pentateuch is, in many respects, the most important in Old Testament history, not only so far as regards Israel, but the Church at all times. Opening with centuries of silence and seeming Divine forgetfulness during the bondage of Egypt, the pride and power of Pharaoh are suddenly broken by a series of miracles, culminating in the deliverance of Israel and the destruction of Egypt's host. In that Paschal night and under the blood-sprinkling, Israel as a nation is born of God, and the redeemed people are then led forth to be consecrated at the Mount by ordinances, laws, and judgments. Finally, we are shown the manner in which Jehovah deals with His people, both in judgment and in mercy, till at the last He safely brings them to the promised inheritance. In all this we see not only the history of the ancient people of God, but also a grand type of the redemption and the sanctification of the Church. There is yet another aspect of it, since this narrative exhibits the foundation of the Church in the Covenant of God, and also the principles of Jehovah's government for all time. For, however great the difference in the development, the essence and character of the covenant of grace are ever the same. The Old and New Testaments are essentially one — not two covenants but one, gradually unfolding into full perfectness, "Jesus Christ Himself being the chief corner stone" of the foundation which is alike that of the apostles and prophets. [1]

There is yet a further consideration besides the intrinsic importance of this history. It has, especially of late, been so boldly misrepresented, and so frequently misunderstood, or else it is so often cursorily read — neither to understanding nor yet to profit — that it seemed desirable to submit it anew to special investigation, following the sacred narrative consecutively from Chapter to Chapter, and almost from Section to Section. In so doing, I have endeavoured to make careful study of the original text, with the help of the best critical appliances. So far as I am conscious, I have not passed by any real difficulty, nor yet left unheeded any question that had a reasonable claim to be answered. If this implied a more detailed treatment, I hope it may also, with God's blessing, render the volume more permanently useful. Further, it has been my aim, by the aid of kindred studies, to shed additional light upon the narrative, so as to render it vivid and pictorial, enabling readers to realise for themselves the circumstances under which an event took place. Thus I have in the first two chapters sought to read the history of Israel in Egypt by the light of its monuments, and also to portray the political, social, and religious state of the people prior to the Exodus. Similarly, when following the wanderings of Israel up to the eastern bank of the Jordan, I have availed myself of the best recent geographical investigations, that so the reader might, as it were, see before him the route followed by Israel, the scenery, and all other accessories.

It need scarcely be said, that in studying this narrative *the open Bible should always be at hand.* But I may remind myself and others, that the only real understanding of any portion of Holy Scripture is that conveyed to the heart by the Spirit of God. And, indeed, throughout, my great object has been, not to supersede the constant and prayerful use of the Bible itself, but rather to lead to those Scriptures, which alone "are able to make wise unto salvation through faith which is in Christ Jesus."

A. E.

Heniach, Bournemouth:
February, 1876.

[1] Eph. ii. 20.

Chapter One

(Exodus 1. 1-7)

The devout Student of history cannot fail to recognise it as a wonderful arrangement of Providence, that the beginning and the close of Divine revelation to mankind were both connected with the highest intellectual culture of the world. When the apostles went forth into the Roman world, they could avail themselves of the Greek language, then universally spoken, of Grecian culture and modes of thinking. And what Greece was to the world at the time of Christ, that and much more had Egypt been when the children of Israel became a God-chosen nation. Not that in either case the truth of God needed help from the wisdom of this world. On the contrary, in one sense, it stood opposed to it. And yet while history pursued seemingly its independent course, and philosophy, science, and the arts advanced apparently without any reference to Revelation, all were in the end made subservient to the furtherance of the kingdom of God. And so it always is. God marvellously uses natural means for supernatural ends, and maketh all things work together to His glory as well as for the good of His people.

It was, indeed, as we now see it, most important that the children of Israel should have been brought into Egypt, and settled there for centuries before becoming an independent nation. The early history of the sons of Jacob must have shown the need alike of their removal from contact with the people of Canaan, and of their being fused in the furnace of affliction, to prepare them for inheriting the land promised unto their fathers. This, however, might have taken place in any other country than Egypt. Not so their training for a nation. For that, Egypt offered the best, or rather, at the time, the only suitable opportunities. True, the stay there involved also peculiar dangers, as their after history proved. But these would have been equally encountered under any other circumstances, while the benefits they derived through intercourse with the Egyptians were peculiar and unique. There is yet another aspect of the matter. When standing before King Agrippa, St. Paul could confidently appeal to the publicity of the history of Christ, as enacted not in some obscure corner of a barbarous land, but in full view of the Roman world: "For this thing was not done in a corner." [1] And so Israel's bondage also and God's marvellous deliverance took place on no less conspicuous a scene than that of the ancient world-empire of Egypt.

Indeed, so close was the connection between Israel and Egypt, that it is impossible properly to understand the history of the former without knowing something of the latter. We shall therefore devote this preliminary chapter to a brief description of Egypt. In general, however historians may differ as to the periods when particular events had taken place, the land itself is full of reminiscences of Israel's story. These have been brought to light by recent researches, which almost year by year add to our stock of knowledge. And here it is specially remarkable, that every fresh historical discovery tends to shed light upon, and to confirm the Biblical narratives. Yet some of the principal arguments against the Bible were at one time derived from the supposed history of Egypt! Thus while men continually raise fresh objections against Holy Scripture, those formerly so confidently relied upon have been removed by further researches, made quite independently of the Bible, just as an enlarged knowledge will sweep away those urged in our days. Already the Assyrian monuments, the stone which records the story of Moab, [2] the temples, the graves, and the ancient papyri of Egypt have been made successively to tell each its own tale, and each marvellously bears out the truth of the Scripture narrative. Let us see what we can learn from such sources of the ancient state of Egypt, so far as it may serve to illustrate the history of Israel.

The connection between Israel and Egypt may be said to have begun with the visit of Abram to that country. On his arrival there he must have found the people already in a high state of civilisation. The history of the patriarch gains fresh light by monuments and old papyri. Thus a papyrus (now in the British Museum), known as *The Two Brothers,* and which is probably the oldest work of fiction in existence, proves that Abram had occasion for fear on account of Sarai. It tells of a Pharaoh, who sent two armies to take a fair woman from her husband and then to murder him. Another papyrus (at present in Berlin) records how the wife and children of a foreigner were taken from him by a Pharaoh. Curiously enough, this papyrus dates from nearly the time when the patriarch was in Egypt. From this period also we have a picture in one of the tombs, representing the arrival of a nomad chief, like Abram, with his family and dependants, who seek the protection of the prince. The newcomer is received as a person of distinction. To make the co-incidence the more striking — though this chief is not thought to have been Abram — he is evidently of Semitic descent, wears a "coat of many colours," is designated *Hyk,* or prince, the equivalent of the modern *Sheich,* or chief of a tribe, and even bears the name of *Ab-shah,* "father of sand," a term resembling that of *Ab-raham,* the "father of a multitude." [3] Another Egyptian story — that of *Sancha,* "the son of the sycomore," — reminds us so far of that of Joseph, that its hero is a foreign nomad, who rises to the highest rank at Pharaoh's court and becomes his chief counsellor. These are instances how Egyptian history illustrates and confirms that of the Bible.

Of the forced employment of the children of Israel in building and repairing certain cities, we have, as will presently be shown, sufficient confirmation in an Egyptian inscription lately discovered. We have also a pictorial representation of Semitic captives, probably Israelites, making bricks in the manner described in the Bible; and yet another, dating from a later reign, in which Israelites — either captives of war, or, as has been recently suggested, mercenaries who had stayed behind after the Exodus — are employed for Pharaoh in drawing stones, or cutting them in the quarries, and in completing or enlarging the fortified city of Rameses, which their fathers had formerly built. The builders delineated in the second of these representations are expressly called *Aperu,* the close correspondence of the name with the designation *Hebrew,* even in its English form, being apparent. Though these two sets of representations date, in all probability, from a period later than the Exodus, they remarkably illustrate what we read of the state and the occupations of the children of Israel during the period of their oppression. Nor does this exhaust the bearing of the Egyptian monuments on the early history of Israel. In fact, we can trace the two histories almost contemporaneously, and see how remarkably the one sheds light upon the other.

In general, our knowledge of Egyptian history is derived from the *monuments,* of which we have already spoken, from certain references in *Greek historians,* which are not of much value, and especially from the historical work of *Manetho,* an Egyptian priest who wrote about the year 250 B.C. At that time the monuments of Egypt were still almost intact. Manetho had access to them all; he was thoroughly conversant with the ancient literature of his country, and he wrote under the direction and patronage of the then monarch of the land. Unfortunately, however, his work has been lost, and the fragments of it preserved exist only in the distorted form which Josephus has given them for his own purposes, and in a chronicle, written by a learned Christian convert of the third century (*Julius Africanus*). But this latter also has been lost, and we know it only from a similar work written a century later (by *Eusebius,* bishop of Caesarea), in which the researches of Africanus are embodied. [4] Such are the difficulties before the student! On the other hand, both Africanus and Eusebius gathered their materials in Egypt itself, and were competent for their task; Africanus, at least, had the work of Manetho before him; and, lastly, by universal consent, the monuments of Egypt remarkably confirm what were the undoubted statements of Manetho. Like most heathen chronologies, Manetho's catalogue of kings begins with gods, after which he enumerates thirty dynasties, bringing the history down to the year 343 B.C. Now some of these dynasties were evidently not successive, but contemporary, that is, they present various lines of kings who at one and the same time ruled over different portions of Egypt. This especially applies to the so-called 7th, 8th, 9th, 10th, and 11th dynasties. It is wholly impossible to conjecture what period of time these may have occupied. After that we have more solid ground. We know that under the 12th dynasty the whole of Egypt was united under one sway. As we gather from the monuments, the country was in a very high state of prosperity and civilisation. At the beginning of this dynasty we suppose the visit of Abram to have taken place. The reign of this 12th dynasty lasted more than two centuries, [5] and either at its close or at the beginning of the 13th dynasty we place the accession and rule of Joseph. From the fourth king of the 13th to the accession of the 18th dynasty Egyptian history is almost a blank. That period was occupied by the rule of the so-called *Hyksos,* or Shepherd kings, a foreign and barbarous race of invaders, hated and opposed by the people, and hostile to their ancient civilisation and religion. Although Josephus represents Manetho as assigning a very long period to the reign of "the Shepherds," he gives only six names. These and these only are corroborated by Egyptian monuments, and we are warranted in inferring that these alone had really ruled over Egypt. The period occupied by their reign might thus amount to between two and three centuries, which agrees with the Scripture chronology.

"The Shepherds" were evidently an eastern race, and probably of Phenician origin. Thus the names of the two first kings in their list are decidedly Semitic (*Salatis*, "mighty," "ruler," and *Beon*, or *Benon*, "the son of the eye," or, the "beloved one"); and there is evidence that the race brought with it the worship of Baal and the practice of human sacrifices — both of Phenician origin. It is important to keep this in mind, as we shall see that there had been almost continual warfare between the Phenicians along the west coast of Palestine and the Hittites, and the native Egyptian kings, who, while they ruled, held them in subjection. This constant animosity also explains why, not without good reason, "every shepherd was an abomination" unto the real native Egyptians. [6] It also explains why the Shepherd kings left the Israelitish shepherds unmolested in the land of Goshen, where they found them. Thus a comparison of Scripture chronology with the history of Egypt, and the evidently peaceful, prosperous state of the country, united under the rule of one king, as described in the Bible, lead us to the conclusion that Joseph's stay there must have taken place at the close of the 12th, or, at latest, at the commencement of the 13th dynasty. He could not have come during the rule of the Hyksos, for then Egypt was in a distracted, divided, and chaotic state; and it could not have been later, for after the Shepherd kings had been expelled and native rulers restored, no "new king," no new dynasty, "arose up over Egypt." On the other hand, the latter description exactly applies to a king who, on his restoration, expelled the Hyksos.

And here the monuments of Egypt again afford remarkable confirmation of the history of Joseph. For one thing, the names of three of the Pharaohs of the 13th dynasty bear a striking resemblance to that given by the Pharaoh of the Bible to Joseph (Zaphnath-paaneah). Then we know that the Pharaohs of the 12th dynasty stood in a very special relationship to the priest city of On, [7] and that its high-priest was most probably always a near relative of Pharaoh. Thus the monuments of that period enable us to understand the history of Joseph's marriage. But they also throw light on a question of far greater importance — how so devout and pious a servant of the Lord as Joseph could have entered into such close relationship with the priesthood of Egypt. Here our knowledge of the most ancient religion of Egypt enables us to furnish a complete answer. Undoubtedly, all mankind had at first some knowledge of the one true God, and a pure religion inherited from Paradise. This primeval religion seems to have been longest preserved in Egypt. Every age indeed witnessed fresh corruptions, till at last that of Egypt became the most abject superstition. But the earliest Egyptian religious records, as preserved in that remarkable work. *The Ritual for the Dead,* disclose a different state of things. There can be no doubt that, divested of all later glosses, they embodied belief in "the unity, eternity, and self-existence of the unknown Deity," in the immortality of the soul, and in future rewards and punishments, and that they inculcated the highest duties of morality. The more closely we study these ancient records of Egypt, the more deeply are we impressed with the high and pure character of its primeval religion and legislation. And when the children of Israel went into the wilderness, they took, in this respect also, with them from Egypt many lessons which had not to be learned anew, though this one grand fundamental truth had to be acquired, that the Deity unknown to the Egyptians was *Jehovah,* the living and the true God. We can therefore understand how such close connection between Joseph and the Egyptian priesthood was both possible and likely.

But this is not all. Only under a powerful native ruler could the redivision of the land and the rearrangement of taxation, which Joseph proposed, have taken place. Moreover, we know that under the rule of the last great king of this native dynasty (the 13th) a completely new system of Nile irrigation *was* introduced, such as we may well believe would have been devised to avoid another period of famine, and, strangest of all, a place by the artificial lake made at that time bears the name *Pi-aneh,* "the house of life," which is singularly like that given by Pharaoh to Joseph. If we now pass over the brief 14th dynasty and the Hyksos period, when we may readily believe Israel remained undisturbed in Goshen, we come to the restoration of a new native dynasty (the so-called 18th). After the "Shepherds" had been expelled, the Israelitish population, remaining behind in the borderland of Goshen, would naturally seem dangerously large to the "new king," the more so as the Israelites were kindred in descent and occupation to the "Shepherds," [8] and had been befriended by them. Under these circumstances a wise monarch might seek to weaken such a population by forced labour. For this purpose he employed them in building fortress-cities, such as Pithom and Raamses. [9] *Raamses* bears the name of the district in which it is situated, but *Pithom* means "the fortress of foreigners," thus indicating its origin. Moreover, we learn from the monuments that this "new king" (Aahmes i.) employed in building his fortresses what are called the *Fenchu* - a word meaning "bearers of the shepherd's staff," and which therefore would exactly describe the Israelites.

The period between the "new king" of the Bible (Aahmes I.) and Thothmes II. (the second in succession to him), when we suppose the Exodus to have taken place, quite agrees with the reckoning of Scripture. Now this Thothmes II. began his reign very brilliantly. But after a while there is a perfect blank in the monumental records about him. But we read of a general revolt after his death among the nations whom his father had conquered. Of course, one could not expect to find on Egyptian monuments an account of the disasters which the nation sustained at the Exodus, nor how Pharaoh and his host had perished in the Red Sea. But we do find in his reign the conditions which we should have expected under such circumstances, viz., a brief, prosperous reign, then a sudden collapse; the king dead; no son to succeed him; the throne occupied by the widow of the Pharaoh, and for twenty years no attempt to recover the supremacy of Egypt over the revolted nations in Canaan and east of the Jordan. Lastly, the character of his queen, as it appears on the monuments, is that of a proud and bitterly superstitious woman, just such as we would have expected to encourage Pharaoh in "hardening his heart" against Jehovah. But the chain of coincidences does not break even here. From the Egyptian documents we learn that in the preceding reign — that is, just before the children of Israel entered the desert of Sinai — the Egyptians ceased to occupy the mines which they had till then worked in that peninsula. Further, we learn that, during the latter part of Israel's stay in the wilderness, the Egyptian king, Thothmes III., carried on and completed his wars in Canaan, and that just immediately before the entry of Israel into Palestine the great confederacy of Canaanitish kings against him was quite broken up. This explains the state in which Joshua found the country, so different from that compact power which forty years before had inspired the spies with such terror; and also helps us to understand how, at the time of Joshua, each petty king just held his own city and district, and how easily the fear of a nation, by which even the dreaded Pharaoh and his host had perished, would fall upon the inhabitants of the land (compare also Balaam's words in Numb. xxiii. 22; xxiv. 8). We may not here follow this connection between the two histories any farther. But all through the troubled period of the early Judges down to Barak and Deborah, Egyptian history, as deciphered from the monuments, affords constant illustration and confirmation of the state of Canaan and the history of Israel, as described in the Bible. Thus did Providence work for the carrying out of God's purposes, and so remarkably does He in our days raise up witnesses for His Word, where their testimony might least have been expected.

We remember that Abram was at the first driven by famine into Egypt. The same cause also led the brothers of Joseph to seek there corn for then: sustenance. For, from the earliest times, Egypt was the great granary of the old world. The extraordinary fertility of the country depends, as is well known, on the annual overflow of the Nile, caused in its turn by rains in the highlands of Abyssinia and Central Africa. So far as the waters of the Nile cover the soil, the land is like a fruitful garden; beyond it all is desolate wilderness. Even in that "land of wonders," as Egypt has been termed, the Nile is one of the grand outstanding peculiarities. Another, as we have seen, consists in its monuments. These two landmarks may conveniently serve to group together what our space will still allow us to say of the country and its people.

The name of the country, Egypt (in Greek *Ai-gyptos*), exactly corresponds to the Egyptian designation *Kah-Ptah,* "the land of Ptah" — one of their gods — and from it the name of *Copts* seems also derived. In the Hebrew Scriptures its name is *Mizraim,* that is, "the two *Mazors,*" which again corresponds with another Egyptian name for the country, *Chem* (the same as "the land of Ham"), [10] both *Mazor* and *Chem* meaning in their respective languages the red mud or dark soil of which the cultivated part of the country consisted. It was called "the two Mazors," probably because of its ancient division into Upper and Lower Egypt. The king of Upper Egypt was designated by a title whose initial sign was a bent reed, which illustrates such passages as 2 Kings xviii. 21; Isaiah xxxvi. 6; Ezekiel xxix. 6; while the rulers of Lower Egypt bore the title of "bee," which may be referred to in Isaiah vii. 18. [11] The country occupies less than 10,000 square geographical miles, of which about 5,600 are at present, and about 8,000 were anciently, fit for cultivation. Scripture history has chiefly to do with Lower Egypt, which is the northern part of the country, while the most magnificent of the monuments are in Upper, or Southern, Egypt.

As already stated, the fertility of the land depends on the overflowing of the Nile, which commences to rise about the middle of June, and reaches its greatest height about the end of September, when it again begins to decrease. As measured at Cairo, if the Nile does not rise twenty-four feet, the harvest will not be very good; anything under eighteen threatens famine. About the middle of August the red, turbid waters of the rising river are distributed by canals over the country, and carry fruitfulness with them. On receding, the Nile leaves behind it a thick red soil, which its waters had carried from Central Africa, and over this rich deposit the seed is sown. Rain there is none, nor is there need for it to fertilise the land. The Nile also furnishes the most pleasant and even nourishing water for drinking, and some physicians have ascribed to it healing virtues. It is scarcely necessary to add that the river teems with fish. Luxuriously rich and green, amidst surrounding desolation, the banks of the Nile and of its numerous canals are like a well-watered garden under a tropical sky. Where climate and soil are the best conceivable, the fertility must be unparalleled. The ancient Egyptians seem to have also bestowed great attention on their fruit and flower gardens, which, like ours, were attached to their villas. On the monuments we see gardeners presenting handsome bouquets; gardens traversed by alleys, and adorned with pavilions and colonnades; orchards stocked with palms, figs, pomegranates, citrons, oranges, plums, mulberries, apricots, etc.; while in the vineyards, as in Italy, the vines were trained to meet across wooden rods, and hang down in rich festoons. Such was the land on which, in the desolate dreariness and famine of the wilderness, Israel was tempted to look back with sinful longing!

When Abram entered Egypt, his attention, like that of the modern traveller, must have been riveted by the Great Pyramids. Of these about sixty have been counted, but the largest are those near the ancient Memphis, which lay about ten miles above Cairo. Memphis — in Scripture Noph [12] — was the capital of Lower, as Thebes that of Upper, Egypt — the latter being the Pathros of Scripture. [13] It is scarcely possible to convey an adequate idea of the pyramids. Imagine a structure covering at the base an area of some 65,000 feet, and slanting upwards for 600 feet; [14] or, to give a better idea than these figures convey, "more than half as long on every side as Westminster Abbey, eighty feet higher than the top of St. Paul's, covering thirteen acres of ground, and computed to have contained nearly seven million tons of solid masonry!" [15] We cannot here enter on the various purposes intended by these wonderful structures, some of which, at any rate, were scientific. Not far from the great pyramids was the ancient On, connected with the history of Joseph, and where Moses probably got his early training. But all hereabout is full of deepest interest — sepulchres, monuments, historical records, and sites of ancient cities. We are in a land of dreams, and all the surroundings bear dreamy outlines; gigantic in their proportions, and rendered even more gigantic by the manner in which they are disposed. Probably the most magnificent of these monuments in Upper Egypt — the Pathros of Scripture — are those of its capital, Thebes, the No, or No Amon of the Bible. [16] It were impossible in brief space to describe its temple. The sanctuary itself was small, but opposite to it a court opened upon a hall into which the great cathedral at Paris might be placed, without touching the walls on either side! One hundred and forty columns support this hall, the central pillars being sixty-six feet high, and so wide that it would take six men with extended arms to embrace one of them. The mind gets almost bewildered by such proportions. All around, the walls bear representations, inscriptions, and records — among others, those of Shishak, who captured Jerusalem during the reign of Rehoboam. But the temple itself is almost insignificant when compared with the approach to it, which was through a double row of sixty or seventy ram-headed sphinxes, placed about eleven feet apart from each other. Another avenue led to a temple which enclosed a lake for funeral rites; and yet a third avenue of sphinxes extended a distance of 6000 feet to a palace. These notices are selected to give some faint idea of the magnificence of Egypt.

It would be difficult to form too high an estimate of the old world culture and civilisation, here laid open before us. The laws of Egypt seem to have been moderate and wise; its manners simple and domestic; its people contented, prosperous, and cultured. Woman occupied a very high place, and polygamy was almost the exception. Science, literature, and the arts were cultivated; commerce and navigation carried on, while a brave army and an efficient fleet maintained the power of the Pharaohs. Altogether the country seems old in its civilisation, when alike the earliest sages of Greece and the lawgivers of Israel learned of its wisdom. But how different the use which Israel was to make of it from that to which the philosophers put their lore! What was true, good, and serviceable was to enter as an element into the life of Israel. But this life was formed and moulded quite differently from that of Egypt. Israel as a nation was born of God; redeemed by God; brought forth by God victorious on the other side the flood; taught of God; trained by God; and separated for the service of God. And this God was to be known to them as Jehovah, the living and the true God. The ideas they had gained, the knowledge they had acquired, the life they had learned, even the truths they had heard in Egypt, might be taken with them, but, as it were, to be baptised in the Red Sea, and consecrated at the foot of Sinai. Quite behind them in the far distance lay the Egypt they had quitted, with its dreamy, gigantic outlines. As the sand carried from the desert would cover the land, so did the dust of superstition gradually bury the old truths. We are ready to admit that Israel profited by what they had seen and learned. But all the more striking is the final contrast between Egyptian superstition, which ultimately degraded itself to make gods of almost everything in nature, and the glorious, spiritual worship of the Israel of God. That contrast meets us side by side with the resemblance to what was in Egypt, and becomes all the more evident by their juxtaposition. Never is the religion of Israel more strikingly the opposite to that of Egypt than where we discover resemblances between the two; and never are their laws and institutions more really dissimilar than when we, trace an analogy between them. Israel may have adopted and adapted much from Egypt, but it *learned* only from the Lord God, who, in every sense of the expression, *brought out* His people with a mighty hand, and an outstretched arm!

[1] Acts xxvi. 26.
[2] 2 Kings iii.
[3] We have here to refer to the masterly essay on "The Bearings of Egyptian History upon the Pentateuch," appended to vol. 1. of what is commonly known as *The Speaker's Commentary*. For an engraving of this remarkable fresco, see *The Land of the Pharaohs: Egypt and Sinai, illustrated by Pen and Pencil,* p. 102 (Religious Tract Society).
[4] Even this exists only in its Armenian translation, not in the original.
[5] We must again refer those who wish fuller information to the essay already mentioned, the conclusions of which we have virtually adopted.

[6] Gen. xlvi. 34.
[7] Gen. xli. 45.
[8] Ex. i. 9, 10.
[9] Ex. i. 11.
[10] Ps. cv. 23, 27.
[11] See also the article "Egypt" in Dr. Smith's *Dictionary of the Bible*.
[12] Is. xix. 13; Jer. ii. 16; xlvi. 14, 19; Ezek. xxx. 13, 16.
[13] Is. xi. 11; Jer. xliv. I, 15.
[14] The perpendicular height is 479 feet.
[15] Canon Trevor, *Ancient Egypt,* p. 40.
[16] Jer. xlvi. 25; Ezek. xxx. 14-16; Nah. iii. 8.

Note on the Book of Exodus

For a clearer understanding, a general outline of the Book of Exodus may here be given. Like Genesis (see *Hist. of the Patriarchs*, Introd. p. xv.), it consists of two great Parts, the first describing the *redemption* of Israel, and the second the consecration of Israel as the *people of God*. The first Part (ch. i.-xv. 21) appropriately ends with "the Song of Moses;" while, similarly, the second Part closes with the erection and consecration of the Tabernacle, in which Jehovah was to dwell in the midst of His people, and to hold fellowship with them.

Again, each of these two Parts may be arranged into seven Sections (*seven* being the covenant number), as follows:

Part I.: I. Preparatory: Israel increases, and is oppressed in Egypt (i.); birth and preservation of a deliverer (ii.);

2. The calling and training of Moses (iii. iv.);

3. His mission to Pharaoh (v.-vii. 7);

4. The signs and wonders (vii. 8-xi.);

5. Israel is set apart by the Passover, and led forth (xii.-xiii. 16);

6. Passage of the Red Sea and destruction of Pharaoh (xiii. 17-xiv.);

7. Song of triumph on the other side (xv. 1-21). The seven sections of Part II. are as follows:

1. March of the children of Israel to the Mount of God (xv. 22-xvii. 7);

2. Twofold attitude of the Gentile nations towards Israel: the enmity of Amalek, and the friendship of Jethro (xvii. 8-xviii.);

3. The covenant at Sinai (xix.-xxiv. 11);

4. Divine directions about making the Tabernacle (xxiv. 12-xxxi.);

5. Apostasy of Israel, and their restoration to be the people of God (xxxii.-xxxiv.);

6. Actual construction of the Tabernacle and of its vessels (xxxv.-xxxix.);

7. The setting up and consecration of the Tabernacle (xl.), the latter corresponding, as closing section of Part II., to the Song of Moses (xv.), with which the first part had ended (see Keil, Bibel Com., vol. i., pp. 302-311).

The reader will note these parts and sections in his Bible, and mark what grandeur and unity there is in the plan of the Book of Exodus, and how fully it realises the idea of telling the story of the kingdom of God.

Chapter Two

(Exodus 1. to end.)

Three centuries and a half intervened between the close of the Book of Genesis and the events with which that of Exodus opens. But during that long period the history of the children of Israel is almost an entire blank. The names of their families have come down to us, but without any chronicle of their history; their final condition at the time of the Exodus is marked, but without any notice of their social or national development. Except for a few brief allusions scattered through the Old Testament, we should know absolutely nothing of their state, their life, or their religion, during all that interval. This silence of three and a half centuries is almost awful in its grandeur, like the loneliness of Sinai, the mount of God.

Two things had been foretold as marking this period, and these two alone appear as outstanding facts in the Biblical narrative. On the boundary of the Holy Land the Lord had encouraged Israel: "Fear not to go down into Egypt;

for I will there make of thee a great nation." [1] And the Book of Exodus opens with the record that this promise had been fulfilled, for "the children of Israel were fruitful, and increased abundantly, and multiplied, and waxed exceeding mighty; and the land was filled with them." [2] Yet another prediction, made centuries before to Abram, was to be fulfilled. His seed was to be "a stranger in a land not theirs," to be enslaved and afflicted. [3] And as the appointed centuries were drawing to a close, there "arose up a new king over Egypt," who "evil entreated our fathers." [4] Thus, in the darkest period of their bondage, Israel might have understood that, as surely as these two predictions had been literally fulfilled, so would the twofold promise also prove true: "I will bring thee up again," and that "with great substance." And here we see a close analogy to the present condition of the Jews. In both cases the promised future stands in marked contrast to the actual state of things. But, like Israel of old, we also have the "more sure word of prophecy," as a "light that shineth in a dark place until the day dawn."

The closing years of the three and a half centuries since their entrance into Egypt found Israel peaceful, prosperous, and probably, in many respects, assimilated to the Egyptians around. "The fathers" had fallen asleep, but their children still held undisturbed possession of the district originally granted them. The land of Goshen, in which they were located, is to this day considered the richest province of Egypt, and could, even now, easily support a million more inhabitants than it numbers. [5] Goshen extended between the most eastern of the ancient seven mouths of the Nile and Palestine. The border-land was probably occupied by the more nomadic branches of the family of Israel, to whose flocks its wide tracts would afford excellent pasturage; while the rich banks along the Nile and its canals were the chosen residence of those who pursued agriculture. Most likely such would also soon swarm across to the western banks of the Nile, where we find traces of them in various cities of the land. [6] There they would acquire a knowledge of the arts and industries of the Egyptians. It seems quite natural that, in a country which held out such inducements for it, the majority of the Israelites should have forsaken their original pursuits of shepherds, and become agriculturists. To this day a similar change has been noticed in the nomads who settle in Egypt. Nor was their new life entirely foreign to their history. Their ancestor, Isaac, had, during his stay among the Philistines, sowed and reaped. [7] Besides, at their settlement in Egypt, the grant of land — and that the best in the country — had been made to them "for a possession," a term implying fixed and hereditary proprietorship. [8] Their later reminiscences of Egypt accord with this view. In the wilderness they looked back with sinful longing to the time when they had cast their nets into the Nile, and drawn them in weighted with fish; and when their gardens and fields by the waterside had yielded rich crops — "the cucumbers, and the melons, and the leeks, and the onions, and the garlick." [9] And afterwards, when Moses described to them the land which they were to inherit, he contrasted its cultivation with their past experience of Egypt, "where thou sowedst thy seed, and wateredst it with thy foot, as a garden of herbs." [10] As further evidence of this change from pastoral to agricultural pursuits, it has also been remarked that, whereas the patriarchs had possessed camels, no allusion is made to them in the narrative of their descendants. No doubt this change of occupation served a higher purpose. For settlement and agriculture imply civilisation, such as was needed to prepare Israel for becoming a nation.

In point of fact, we have evidence that they had acquired most of the arts and industries of ancient Egypt. The preparation of the various materials for the Tabernacle, as well as its construction, imply this. Again, we have such direct statements, as, for example, that some of the families of Judah were "carpenters" [11] (1 Chron. iv. 14), "weavers of fine Egyptian linen" (ver. 21), and "potters" (ver. 23). These must, of course, be regarded as only instances of the various trades learned in Egypt. Nor was the separation between Israel and the Egyptians such as to amount to isolation. Goshen would, of course, be chiefly, but not exclusively, inhabited by Israelites. These would mingle even in the agricultural districts, but, naturally, much more in the towns, with their Egyptian neighbours. Accordingly, it needed the Paschal provision of the blood to distinguish the houses of the Israelites from those of the Egyptians; [12] while Exodus iii. 22 seems to imply that they were not only neighbours, but perhaps, occasionally, residents in the same houses. This also accounts for the "mixed multitude" that accompanied Israel at the Exodus, and, later on, in the wilderness, for the presence in the congregation of offspring from marriages between Jewish women and Egyptian husbands. [13]

While the greater part of Israel had thus acquired the settled habits of a nation, the inhabitants of the border-district between Goshen and Canaan continued their nomadic life. This explains how the tribes of Reuben, Gad, and Manasseh possessed so much larger flocks than their brethren, as afterwards to claim the wide pasture-lands to the east of Jordan. [14] We have, also, among the records of "ancient stories," [15] a notice of some of the descendants of Judah exercising lordship in Moab, and we read of a predatory incursion into Gath on the part of some of the descendants of Ephraim, which terminated fatally. [16] It is but fair to assume that these are only instances, mentioned, the one on account of its signal success, the other on that of its failure, and that both imply nomadic habits and incursions into Canaan on the part of those who inhabited the border-land.

But whether nomadic or settled, Israel preserved its ancient *constitution* and *religion,* though here also we notice modifications and adaptations, arising from their long settlement in Egypt The original division of Israel was into twelve tribes, after the twelve sons of Jacob, an arrangement which continued, although the sons of Joseph became two tribes (Ephraim and Manasseh), since the priestly tribe of Levi had no independent political standing. These twelve tribes were again subdivided into *families* (or rather clans), mostly founded by the grandsons of Jacob, of which we find a record in

18

Numb. xxvi., and which amounted in all to sixty. From Joshua vii. 14 we learn that those "families" had at that time, if not earlier, branched into "households," and these again into what is described by the expression "man by man" (in the Hebrew, *Gevarim*). The latter term, however, is really equivalent to our "family," as appears from a comparison of Josh. vii. 14 with vers. 17, 18. Thus we have in the oldest times *tribes* and *clans,* and in those of Joshua, if not earlier, the clans again branching into *households* (kin) and *families.* The "heads" of those clans and families were their chiefs; those of the *tribes,* "the princes." [17] These twelve princes were "the rulers of the congregation." [18] By the side of these rulers, who formed a *hereditary aristocracy,* we find two classes of *elective officials,* [19] as "representatives" of "the congregation." [20] These are designated in Deut. xxix. 10, as the "elders" and the "officers," or, rather, "scribes." Thus the rule of the people was jointly committed to the "princes," the "elders," and the "officers." [21] The institution of "elders" and of "scribes" had already existed among the children of Israel in Egypt before the time of Moses. For Moses "gathered the elders of Israel together," to announce to them his Divine commission, [22] and through them he afterwards communicated to the people the ordinance of the Passover. [23] The mention of "scribes" as "officers" occurs even earlier than that of elders, and to them, as the lettered class, the Egyptian taskmasters seem to have entrusted the superintendence of the appointed labours of the people. [24] From the monuments of Egypt we know what an important part "the scribes" played in that country, and how constantly their mention recurs. Possibly, the order of scribes may have been thus introduced among Israel. As the lettered class, the scribes would naturally be the intermediaries between their brethren and the Egyptians. We may, therefore, regard them also as the representatives of learning, alike Israelitish and Egyptian. That the art of writing was known to the Israelites at the time of Moses is now generally admitted. Indeed, Egyptian learning had penetrated into Canaan itself, and Joshua found its inhabitants mostly in a very advanced state of civilisation, one of the towns bearing even the name of *Kirjath-sepher,* the city of books, or *Kirjath-sannah,* which might almost be rendered "university town." [25]

In reference to the *religion* of Israel, it is important to bear in mind that, during the three and a half centuries since the death of Jacob, all direct communication from Heaven, whether by prophecy or in vision, had, so far as we know, wholly ceased. Even the birth of Moses was not Divinely intimated. In these circumstances the children of Israel were cast upon that knowledge which they had acquired from "the fathers," and which, undoubtedly, was preserved among them. It need scarcely be explained, although it shows the wisdom of God's providential arrangements, that the simple patriarchal forms of worship would suit the circumstances in Egypt much better than those which the religion of Israel afterwards received. *Three great observances* here stand out prominently. Around them the faith and the worship alike of the ancient patriarchs, and afterwards of Israel, may be said to have clustered. They are: circuvicision, *sacrifices,* and the *Sabbath.* We have direct testimony that the rite of circumcision was observed by Israel in Egypt." [26] As to *sacrifices,* even the proposal to celebrate a great sacrificial feast in the wilderness, [27] implies that sacrificial worship had maintained its hold upon the people. Lastly, the direction to gather on the Friday two days' provision of manna, [28] and the introduction of the Sabbath command by the word "Remember," [29] convey the impression of previous *Sabbath observance* on the part of Israel. Indeed, the manner in which many things, as, for example, the practice of vows, are spoken of in the law, seems to point back to previous religious rites among Israel.

Thus far for those outward observances, which indicate how, even during those centuries of silence and loneliness in Egypt, Israel still cherished the fundamental truths of their ancestral religion. But there is yet another matter, bearing reference not to their articles of belief or to observances, but to the religious life of the family and of individuals in Israel. This appears in the *names* given by parents to their children during the long and hard bondage of Egypt. It is well known what significance attaches in the Old Testament to *names.* Every spiritually important event gave its new and characteristic name to a person or locality. Sometimes — as in the case of Abram, Sarai, and Jacob — it was God Himself Who gave such new name; at others, it was the expression of hearts that recognised the special and decisive interposition of God, or else breathed out their hopes and experiences, as in the case of Moses' sons. But any one who considers such frequently recurring names among "the princes" of Israel, as *Eliasaph* (my God that gathers), *Elizur* (my God a rock), and others of kindred import, will gather how deep the hope of Israel had struck its roots in the hearts and convictions of the people. This point will be further referred to in the sequel. Meantime, we only call attention to the names of the chiefs of the three families of the Levites: *Eliasaph* (my God that gathers), *Elizaphan* (my God that watcheth all around), and *Zuriel* (my rock is God)— the Divine Name (*El*) being the same by which God had revealed Himself to the fathers.

Besides their own inherited rites, the children of Israel may have learned many things from the Egyptians, or been strengthened in them. And here, by the side of resemblance, we also observe marked contrast between them. We have already seen that, originally, the religion of the Egyptians had contained much of truth, which, however, was gradually perverted to superstition. The Egyptians and Israel might hold the same truths, but with the difference of understanding and application between dim tradition and clear Divine revelation. Thus, both Israel and the Egyptians believed in the great doctrines of the immortality of the soul, and of future rewards and punishments. But, in connection with this, Israel was taught another lesson, far more difficult to our faith, and which the ancient Egyptians had never learned, that God is the God of the *present* as well as of the future, and that even here on earth He *reigneth,* dispensing good and evil. And perhaps it was owing to this that the temporal consequences of sin were so much insisted upon in the Mosaic law. There was no special need to refer to the consequences in another life. The Egyptians, as well as Israel, acknowledged the latter, but the Egyptians knew not the former. Yet this new truth would teach Israel constantly to realise Jehovah as the living and the true God. On the other hand, the resemblances between certain institutions of Israel and of Egypt clearly prove that the Law was not given at a later period, but to those who came out from Egypt, and immediately upon their leaving it. At the same time, much evil was also acquired by intercourse with the Egyptians. In certain provisions of the Pentateuch we discover allusions, not only to the moral corruptions witnessed, and perhaps learned, in Egypt, but also to the idolatrous practices common there. Possibly, it was not the gorgeous ritual of Egypt which made such deep impression, but the services constantly there witnessed may have gradually accustomed the mind to the worship of nature. As instances of this tendency among Israel, Ave remember the worship of the golden calf, [30] the warning against sacrificing unto the "he-goat," [31] and the express admonition, even of Joshua (xxiv. 14), to "put away the strange gods" which their "fathers served on the other side of the flood." To the same effect is the retrospect in Ezek. xx. 5-8, in Amos v. 26, and in the address of Stephen before the Jewish council. [32] Yet it is remarkable that, although the forms of idolatry here referred to were all practised in Egypt, there is good reason for believing that they were not, so to speak, strictly Egyptian in their origin, but rather foreign rites imported, probably from the Phenicians. [33]

Such then was the political, social, and religious state of Israel, when their long peace was suddenly interrupted by tidings that Aahmes I. was successfully making war against the foreign dynasty of the Hyksos. Advancing victoriously, he at last took Avaris, the great stronghold and capital of the Shepherd kings, and expelled them and their adherents from the country. He then continued his progress to the borders of Canaan, taking many cities by storm. The memorials of the disastrous rule of the Shepherds were speedily removed; the worship which they had introduced was abolished, and the old Egyptian forms were restored. A reign of great prosperity now ensued.

Although there is difference of opinion on the subject, yet every likelihood (as shown in the previous chapter) seems to attach to the belief that the accession of this new dynasty was the period when the "king arose who knew not Joseph." [34] For reasons already explained, one of the first and most important measures of his internal administration would necessarily be to weaken the power of the foreign settlers, who were in such vast majority in the border province of Goshen. He dreaded lest, in case of foreign war, they might join the enemy, "and get them up out of the land." The latter apprehension also shows that the king must have known the circumstances under which they had at first settled in the land. Again, from the monuments of Egypt, it appears to have been at all times the policy of the Pharaohs to bring an immense number of captives into Egypt, and to retain them there in servitude for forced labours. A somewhat similar policy was now pursued towards Israel. Although allowed to retain their flocks and fields, they were set to hard labour for the king. Egyptian "taskmasters" were appointed over them, who "made the children of Israel serve with rigour," and did "afflict them with their burdens." A remarkable illustration of this is seen in one of the Egyptian monuments. Labourers, who are evidently foreigners, and supposed to represent Israelites, are engaged in the various stages of brickmaking, under the superintendence of four Egyptians, two of whom are apparently superior officers, while the other two are overseers armed with heavy lashes, who cry out, "Work without fainting!" The work in which the Israelites were employed consisted of brickmaking, artificial irrigation of the land, including, probably, also the digging or restoring of canals, and the building, or restoring and enlarging of the two "magazine-cities" [35] of Pithom and Raamses, whose localities have been traced in Goshen, and which served as depots both for commerce and for the army. According to Greek historians it was the boast of the Egyptians that, in their great works, they only employed captives and slaves, never their own people. But Aahmes I. had special need of Israelitish labour, since we learn from an inscription, dating from his twenty-second year, that he was largely engaged in restoring the temples and buildings destroyed by the "Shepherds."

But this first measure of the Pharaohs against Israel produced the opposite result from what had been expected. So far from diminishing, their previous vast growth went on in increased ratio, so that the Egyptians "were sorely afraid [36] (alarmed) because of the children of Israel." [37] Accordingly Pharaoh resorted to a second measure, by which all male children, as they were born, were to be destroyed, probably unknown to their parents. But the two Hebrew women, who, as we suppose, were at the head of "the guild" of midwives, do not seem to have communicated the king's order to their subordinates. At any rate, the command was not executed. Scripture has preserved the names of these courageous women^ and told us that their motive was "fear of God" (in the Hebrew with the article, "the God," as denoting the living and true God). And as they were the means of "making" or upbuilding the houses of Israel, so God "made them houses." It is true that, when challenged by the king, they failed to speak out their true motive; but, as St. Augustine remarks, "God forgave the evil on account of the good, and rewarded their piety, though not their deceit."

How little indeed any merely human device could have averted the ruin of Israel, appears from the third measure which Pharaoh now adopted. Putting aside every restraint, and forgetting, in his determination, even his interests, the king issued a general order to cast every Jewish male child, as it was born, into the Nile. Whether this command, perhaps given in anger, was not enforced for any length of time, or the Egyptians were unwilling permanently to lend themselves to such cruelty, or the Israelites found means of preserving their children from this danger, certain it is, that, while many must have suffered, and all needed to use the greatest precautions, this last ruthless attempt to exterminate Israel also proved vain.

Thus the two prophecies *had* been fulfilled. Even under the most adverse circumstances Israel had so increased as to fill the Egyptians with alarm; and the "affliction" of Israel had reached its highest point. And now the promised deliverance was also to appear. As in so many instances, it came in what men would call the most unlikely manner.

[1] Gen. xlvi. 3.

[2] Ex. i. 7.

[3] Gen. xv. 13-16.

[4] Acts vii. 19.

[5] Robinson's *Bibl. Res.* (2nd ed.) vol. i., p. 54.

[6] Ex. xii.

[7] Gen. xxvi. 12.

[8] Gen. xlvii. ii, 27.

[9] Numb. xi. 5.

[10] Deut. xi. 10.

[11] The reference is probably to "guilds," such as in Egypt. The word rendered in our Authorised Version "craftsmen," means "carpenters."

[12] Ex. xii. 13.

[13] Ley xxiv. 10.

[14] Numb. xxxii. 1-4.

[15] 1 Chron. iv. 22.

[16] 1 Chron. vii. 21 is involved and difficult. But the best critics have understood it as explained in the text.

[17] Numb. i. 4, 16, 44; ii. 3, etc.; vii. 10.

[18] Ex. xxxiv. 31; Numb. vii. 2; xxx. I; xxxi. 13; xxxii. 2; xxxiv. 18.

[19] Comp. Deu. i. 9-14.

[20] Numb. xxvii. 2.

[21] See also Deut. xxxi. 28. In the wilderness a meeting of these three classes of rulers seems to have been called by blowing the two silver trumpets, while blasts from one summoned only a council of the princes (Numb. x. 3, 4). It deserves special notice that this mixed rule of hereditary and elective officids continued the constitutional government of the people, not only during the period of the Judges, but under the Kings. We find its analogy also in the rule of the Synagogue.

[22] Ex. iii. 16; iv. 29.

[23] Ex. xii. 21.

[24] Ex. v. 6, 14 15, 19.

[25] Josh. xv. 15, 49.

[26] Ex. iv. 24-26; Josh. v. 5.

[27] Ex. viii. 25-28.

[28] Ex. xvi. 22.

[29] Ex. xx. 8.

[30] Ex. xxxii.

[31] Lev. xvii. 7. Erroneously rendered in our Authorised Version "devils."

[32] Acts vii. 43.

[33] This is very ably argued by Mr. R. J. Poole in Smith's *Dict. of the Bible,* vol. iii. "Remphan."

[34] The Hebrew word "arose" is almost always used to describe a new commencement (as in Deut. xxxiv. 10); the word "new" occurs in connection with an entire change (as in Deut. xxxii. 17; Judges v. 8), while the expression, "knew not" (Deut. xxviii. 36) is applied not so much to absolute want of knowledge, as to the absence of *friendly* acquaintanceship. If this king began a new dynasty, he must have been either the first of the Hyksos or else of those who expelled them. As the former assumption is almost impossible, we are shut up to the latter.

[35] This, and not "treasure-cities," is the literal rendering.

[36] The expression is the same as in Numb. xxii. 3, and implies "to be struck with awe."

[37] Ex. i. 12.

Chapter Three

(Exodus ii.)

To the attentive reader of Scripture it will not seem strange — only remarkable — that the very measure which Pharaoh had taken for the destruction of Israel eventually led to their deliverance. Had it not been for the command to cast the Hebrew children into the river, Moses would not have been rescued by Pharaoh's daughter, nor trained in all the wisdom of Egypt to fit him for his calling. Yet all throughout, this marvellous story pursues a *natural* course; that is, natural in its progress, but supernatural in its purposes and results.

A member of the tribe of Levi, and descendant of Kohath, [1] *Amram* by name, had married *Jochebed,* who belonged to the same tribe. Their union had already been blessed with two children, Miriam and Aaron, [2] when the murderous edict of Pharaoh was issued. The birth of their next child brought them the more sorrow and care, that the "exceeding fairness" of the child not only won their hearts, but seemed to point him out as destined of God for some special purpose. [3] In this struggle of affection and hope against the fear of man, they obtained the victory, as victory is always obtained, "by faith." There was no special revelation made to them, nor was there need for it. It was a simple question of faith, weighing the command of Pharaoh against the command of God and their own hopes. They resolved to trust the living God of their fathers, and to brave all seeming danger. It was in this sense that "by faith Moses, when he was born, was hid three months of his parents, because they saw he was a proper child, and they were not afraid of the king's commandment." Longer concealment at home being impossible, the same confidence of faith now led the mother to lay the child in an ark made, as at that time the light Nile-boats used to be, of "bulrushes," or papyrus — a strong three-cornered rush, that grew to a height of about ten or fifteen feet. [4] The "ark" — a term used in Scripture only here and in connection with the deliverance of Noah by an "ark" — was made tight within by "slime" — either Nilemud or asphalt — and impenetrable to water by a coating of "pitch." Thus protected, the "ark," with its precious burden, was deposited among "the flags" in the brink, or lip of the river, just where Pharaoh's daughter was wont to bathe, though the sacred text does not expressly inform us whether or not this spot was purposely chosen.

The allusion in Ps. lxxviii. 12, to the "marvellous things" done "in the field of Zoan," may perhaps guide us to the very scene of this deliverance. Zoan, as we know, was the ancient *Avaris,* the capital of the Shepherd kings, which the new dynasty had taken from them. The probability that it would continue the residence of the Pharaohs, the more so as it lay on the eastern boundary of Goshen, is confirmed by the circumstance that in those days, of all the ancient Egyptian residences, Avaris or Zoan alone lay on an arm of the Nile which was not infested by crocodiles, and where the princess therefore could bathe. There is a curious illustration on one of the Egyptian monuments of the scene described in the rescue of Moses. A noble lady is represented bathing in the river with four of her maidens attending upon her, just like the daughter of Pharaoh in the story of Moses. But to return — the discovery of the ark, and the weeping of the babe, as the stranger lifted him, are all true to nature. The princess is touched by the appeal of the child to her woman's feelings. She compassionates him none the less that he is one of the doomed race. To have thrown the weeping child into the river would have been inhuman. Pharaoh's daughter acted as every woman would have done in the circumstances. [5] To save *one* Hebrew child could be no very great crime in the king's daughter. Moreover, curiously enough, we learn from the monuments, that just at that very time the royal princesses exercised special influence — in fact, that two of them were co-regents. So when, just at the opportune moment, Miriam, who all along had watched at a little distance, came forward and proposed to call some Hebrew woman to nurse the weeping child — this strange gift, bestowed as it were by the Nile-god himself on the princess, [6] — she readily consented. The nurse called was, of course, the child's own mother, who received her babe now as a precious charge, entrusted to her care by the daughter of him who would have compassed his destruction. So marvellous are the ways of God.

One of the old church-writers has noted that "the daughter of Pharaoh is the community of the Gentiles," thereby meaning to illustrate this great truth, which we trace throughout history, that somehow the salvation of Israel was always connected with the instrumentality of the Gentiles. It was so in the history of Joseph, and even before that; audit will continue so till at the last, through their mercy, Israel shall obtain mercy. But meanwhile a precious opportunity was afforded to those believing Hebrew parents to mould the mind of the adopted son of the princess of Egypt. The three first years of life, the common eastern time for nursing, are often, even in our northern climes, where development is so much slower, a period decisive in after life. It requires no stretch of imagination to conceive what the child Moses would learn at his mother's knee, and hear among his persecuted people. When a child so preserved and so trained found himself destined to step from his Hebrew home to the court of Pharaoh - his mind full of the promises made to the fathers, and his heart heavy with the sorrows of his brethren, - it seems almost natural that thoughts of future deliverance of his people through him should gradually rise in his soul. Many of our deepest purposes have their root in earliest childhood, and the lessons then learnt, and the thoughts then conceived, have been steadily carried out to the end of our lives.

Yet, as in all deepest life-purpose, there was no rashness about carrying it into execution. When Jochebed brought the child back to the princess, the latter gave her adopted son the Egyptian name "Moses," which, curiously enough, appears also in several of the old Egyptian papyri, among others, as that of one of the royal princes. The word means "brought forth," or "drawn out," "because," as she said in giving the name, "I drew him out of the water." [7] But for the present Moses would probably not reside in the royal palace at Avaris. St. Stephen tells us [8] that he "was instructed in all the wisdom of the Egyptians." In no country was such value attached to education, nor was it begun so early as in Egypt. No sooner was a child weaned than it was sent to school, and instructed by regularly appointed scribes. As writing was not by letters, but by hieroglyphics, which might be either pictorial representations, or symbols (a sceptre for a king, etc.), or a kind of phonetic signs, and as there seem to have been hieroglyphics for single letters, for syllables, and for words, that art alone must, from its complication, have taken almost a lifetime to master it perfectly. But beyond this, education was carried to a very great length, and, in the case of those destined for the higher professions, embraced not only the various sciences, as mathematics, astronomy, chemistry, medicine, etc., but theology, philosophy, and a knowledge of the laws. There can be no doubt that, as the adopted son of the princess, Moses would receive the highest training. Scripture tells us that, in consequence, he was "mighty in his words and deeds," and we may take the statement in its simplicity, without entering upon the many Jewish and Egyptian legends which extol his wisdom, and his military and other achievements.

Thus the first forty years of Moses' life passed. Undoubtedly, had he been so minded, a career higher even than that of Joseph might have been open to him. But, before entering it, he had to decide that one great preliminary question, with whom he would cast in his lot — with Egypt or with Israel, with the world or the promises. As so often happens, the providence of God here helped him to a clear, as the grace of God to a right, decision. In the actual circumstances of Hebrew persecution it was impossible at the same time "to be called the son of Pharaoh's daughter" and to have part, as one of them, "with the people of God." The one meant "the pleasures of sin" and "the treasures of Egypt" — enjoyment and honours, the other implied "affliction" and "the reproach of Christ" — or suffering and that obloquy which has always attached to Christ and to His people, and at that time especially, to those who clung to the covenant of which Christ was the substance.

But "faith," which is "the substance of things hoped for, the evidence of things not seen," enabled Moses not only to "refuse" what Egypt held out, but to "choose rather the affliction," and, more than that, to "esteem the reproach of Christ greater riches than the treasures of Egypt," because "he had respect unto the recompence of the reward." [9] In this spirit "he went out unto his brethren, and looked on their burdens." [10] But his faith was, though deeply genuine, as yet far from pure and spiritual. The ancient Egyptians were noted for the severity of their discipline, and their monuments represent the "taskmasters" armed with heavy scourges, made of tough bending wood, which they unmercifully used. The sight of such sufferings, inflicted by menials upon his brethren, would naturally rouse the utmost resentment of the son of the Princess Royal. This, together with the long-cherished resolve to espouse the cause of his brethren, and the nascent thought of becoming their deliverer, led him to slay an Egyptian, whom he saw thus maltreating "an Hebrew, one of his brethren." Still it was not an access of sudden frenzy, for "he looked this way and that way," to see "that there was no man" to observe his deed; rather was it an attempt to carry out spiritual ends by carnal means, such as in the history of Moses' ancestors had so often led to sin and suffering. He would become a deliverer before he was called to it of God; and he would accomplish it by other means than those which God would appoint. One of the fathers has rightly compared this deed to that of Peter in cutting off the ear of the high-priest's servant; at the same time also calling attention to the fact, that the heart both of Moses and Peter resembled a field richly covered with weeds, but which by their very luxuriance gave promise of much good fruit, when the field should have been broken up and sown with good seed.

In the gracious dispensation of God, that time had now come. Before being transplanted, so to speak, Moses had to be cut down. He had to strike root downwards, before he could spring upwards. As St. Stephen puts it, "his brethren understood not how that God, by his hand, would give them deliverance" — what his appearance and conduct among them really meant; and when next he attempted to interfere in a quarrel between two Hebrews, the wrong-doer in harsh terms disowned his authority, and reproached him with his crime. It was now evident that the matter was generally known. Presently it reached the ears of Pharaoh. From what we know of Egyptian society, such an offence could not have remained unpunished, even in the son of a princess, and on the supposition that she who had originally saved Moses was still alive, after the lapse of forty years, and that the then reigning Pharaoh was her father. But, besides, Moses had not only killed an official in the discharge of his duty, he had virtually taken the part of the Hebrews, and encouraged them to rebellion. That Moses commanded such position of influence that Pharaoh could not at once order his execution, but "sought to slay him," only aggravated the matter, and made Moses the more dangerous. Open resistance to Pharaoh was of course impossible. The sole hope of safety now seemed to lie in renouncing all further connection with his people. That or, flight were the only alternatives. On the other hand, flight might further provoke the wrath of the king, and it was more than doubtful whether any of the neighbouring countries could, under such circumstances, afford him safe shelter. It was therefore, indeed, once more an act of "faith" when Moses "forsook Egypt, not fearing the wrath of the king, for he endured" (or remained stedfast, viz., to his choice and people), "as seeing the Invisible One," that is, as one who, instead of considering the king of Egypt, looked by faith to the King invisible. [11]

Like Jacob of old, and Joseph under similar circumstances, Moses must now go into a strange land. All that Egypt could teach him, he *had* acquired. What he still needed could only be learned in lowliness, humiliation, and suffering.

Two things would become manifest in the course of his history. That which, in his own view, was to have freed his people from their misery, had only brought misery to himself On the other hand, that which seemed to remove him from his special calling, would prepare the way for its final attainment. And so it often happens to us in the most important events of our lives, that thus we may learn the lessons of faith and implicit self-surrender, and that God alone may have the glory.

Disowned by his people, and pursued by the king, the gracious Providence of God prepared a shelter and home for the fugitive. Along the eastern shore of the Red Sea the Midianites, descended from Abraham through Keturah, [12] had their settlements, whence, as nomads, they wandered, on one side to the southern point of the peninsula of Sinai, and on the other, northward, as far as the territory of Moab. Among the Midianites it happened to Moses, as of old to Jacob on his flight. At the "well" he was able to protect the daughters of Reuel, "the priest of Midian," against the violence of the shepherds, who drove away their flocks. [13] Invited in consequence to the house of Reuel, he continued there, and eventually married Zipporah, the daughter of the priest. This, and the birth of his two sons, to which we shall presently refer, is absolutely all that Moses himself records of his forty years' stay in Midian.

But we are in circumstances to infer some other and important details. The father-in-law of Moses seems to have worshipped the God of Abraham, as even his name implies: *Reuel,* the "friend of El," being the designation which the patriarchs gave to God, as *El Shaddai,* "God Almighty." [14] This is further borne out by his after-conduct. [15] Reuel is also called *Jethro* and *Jether,* [16] which means "excellency," and was probably his official title as chief priest of the tribe, the same as the *Imam* of the modern Arabs, the term having a kindred meaning. [17] But the life of Moses in the house of Reuel must have been one of humiliation and lowliness. From her after-conduct [18] we infer that Zipporah was a woman of violent, imperious temper, who had but little sympathy with the religious convictions of her husband. When she first met him as "an Egyptian," his bravery may have won her heart. But further knowledge of the deepest aims of his life might lead her to regard him as a gloomy fanatic, who busied his mind with visionary schemes. So little indeed does she seem to have had in common with her husband that, at the most trying and noble period of his life, when on his mission to Pharaoh, he had actually to send her away. [19] Nor could there have been much confidence between Moses and his father-in-law. His very subordinate position in the family of Jethro (iii. i); the fact of his reticence in regard to the exact vision vouchsafed him of God (iv. 18); and the humble manner in which Moses was sent back into Egypt (ver. 20), all give a saddening view of the mutual relations. What, however, all this time were the deepest feelings and experiences of his heart, found expression in the names which he gave to his two sons. The elder he named *Gershom* (expulsion, banishment), [20] "for he said, I have been a stranger in a strange land;" [21] the second he called *Eliezer*, "my God is help" (xviii. 4). Banished to a strange land, far from his brethren and the land of promise, Moses longs for his real home. Yet this feeling issues not in despondency, far less in disbelief or distrust. On the contrary, "the peaceable fruits of righteousness," springing from the "chastening" of the Lord, appear in the name of his second son; "for the God of my fathers," said he, "is mine help, and delivered me from the sword of Pharaoh." The self-confidence and carnal zeal manifest in his early attempt to deliver his brethren in Egypt have been quenched in the land of his banishment, and in the school of sorrow. And the result of all he has suffered and learned has been absolute trustfulness in the God of his fathers, the God of the promises, Who would surely fulfil His word.

[1] Ex. vi. 20; Numb. xxvi. 59.

[2] The narrative implies that they were born before the murderous edict. Aaron was three years older than Moses (Ex. vii. 7), while Miriam was grown up when Moses was exposed (Ex. ii. 4).

[3] The expression in Acts vii. 20 is "fair before God."

[4] Everything here is strictly Egyptian; even some of the terms used in the Hebrew are derived from the Egyptian. The papyrus no longer grows below Nubia, but the Egyptian monuments exhibit many such "arks" and boats made of the plant, and similarly prepared. The "flags" were a smaller species of papyrus.

[5] In what is commonly known as *The Speaker's Commentary*, an illustration of this is given from the so-called *Ritual for the Dead*, the most ancient existing religious record of Egypt. It seems that one of the things which the disembodied spirit had to answer before the Lord of truth was this: "I have not afflicted any man; I have not made any man weep; I have not withheld milk from the mouth of sucklings."

[6] The Egyptians worshipped the Nile as a god.

[7] Others have derived it from two old Egyptian words which literally mean, "water," "saved."

[8] Acts vii. 22.

[9] Heb. xi. 24-26.

[10] Ex. ii. 11.

[11] I Tim. i. 17.

[12] Gen. xxv. 2-4.

[13] Both in Ex. ii. 16, and iii, I, the Hebrew expression for "flocks" implies that they consisted of sheep and goats, not of cattle, and thus affords another indirect testimony to the truth of the narrative, as only such flocks would be ordinarily pastured in that district.

[14] Ex. vi. 3.

[15] Ex. xviii.

[16] Ex. iii. I; iv. 18.

[17] We must distinguish *Reuel* Jethro from Hobab, who seems to have been the son of Reuel, and brother-in-law of Moses, and to have accompanied Israel on their journey (see Judges iv. ii). There is a little difficulty here, as the word rendered in our Authorised Version "father-in-law," really means every relative by marriage.

[18] Ex. iv. 25.

[19] Ex. xviii. 2, 3.

[20] Mr. Cook regards it as a compound of a Hebrew and an Egyptian word meaning "a stranger" in "a foreign land."

[21] Ex. ii. 22.

Chapter Four

(Exodus ii. 23; iv. 17.)

When God is about to do any of His great works, He first silently prepares all for it. Not only the good seed to be scattered, but the breaking up of the soil for its reception is His. Instrumentalities, unrecognised at the time, are silently at work; and, together with the good gift to be bestowed on His own. He grants them the felt need and the earnest seeking of it. Thus prayers and answers are, as it were, the scales of grace in equipoise.

It was not otherwise when God would work the great deliverance of His people from Egypt. Once more it seemed as if the clouds overhead were just then darkest and heaviest. One king had died and another succeeded; [1] but the change of government brought not to Israel that relief which they had probably expected. Their bondage seemed now part of the settled policy of the Pharaohs. Not one ray of hope lit up their sufferings other than what might have been derived from faith. But centuries had passed without any communication or revelation from the God of their fathers! It must therefore be considered a revival of religion when, under such circumstances, the people, instead of either despairing or plotting rebellion against Pharaoh, turned in earnest prayer unto the Lord, or, as the sacred text puts it, significantly adding the definite article before God, [2] "cried" "unto the God," that is, not as unto one out of many, but unto the only true and living God. This spirit of prayer, now for the first time appearing among them, was the first pledge and harbinger, indeed, the commencement of their deliverance. [3] For though only "a cry," so to speak, spiritually inarticulate, no intervening period of time divided their prayer from its answer. "And God heard their groaning, and God remembered His covenant with Abraham, with Isaac, and with Jacob. And God looked upon the children of Israel, and God had respect unto them" — literally, He "knew them," that is, recognised them as the chosen seed of Abraham, and, recognising, manifested His love towards them.

The southern end of the peninsula of Sinai, to which the sacred narrative now takes us, consists of a confused mass of peaks (the highest above 9,000 feet), some of dark green porphyry, but mostly red granite of different hues, which is broken by strips of sand or gravel, intersected by wádies or glens, which are the beds of winter torrents, and dotted here and there with green spots, chiefly due to perennial fountains. The great central group among these mountains is that of Horeb, and one special height in it Sinai, the "mount of God." Strangely enough, it is just here amidst this awful desolateness that the most fertile places in "the wilderness" are also found. Even in our days some of this plateau is quite green. Hither the Bedouin drive their flocks when summer has parched all the lower districts. Fruit-trees grow in rich luxuriance in its valleys, and "the neighbourhood is the best watered in the whole peninsula, running streams being found in no less than four of the adjacent valleys." [4] It was thither that Moses, probably in the early summer, [5] drove Reuel's flock for pasturage and water. Behind him, to the east, lay the desert; before him rose in awful grandeur the mountain of God. The stillness of this place is unbroken; its desolateness only relieved by the variety of colouring in the dark green or the red mountain peaks, some of which "shine in the sunlight like burnished copper." The atmosphere is such that the most distant outlines stand out clearly defined, and the faintest sound falls distinctly on the ear. All at once truly a "strange sight" presented itself. On a solitary crag, or in some sequestered valley, one of those spiked, gnarled, thorny acacia trees, which form so conspicuous a feature in the wadies of "the desert," of which indeed they are "the only timber tree of any size," [6] stood enwrapped in fire, and yet "the bush was not consumed." At view of this, Moses turned aside "to see this great sight." And yet greater wonder than this awaited him. A vision which for centuries had not been seen now appeared; a voice which had been silent these many ages again spoke. "The Angel of Jehovah" (ver. 2), who is immediately afterwards Himself called "Jehovah" and "God" (vers. 4, 5), spake to him "out of the midst of the bush." His first words warned Moses to put his shoes from off his feet, as standing on holy ground; the next revealed Him as the same Angel of the Covenant, who had appeared unto the fathers as "the God of Abraham, the God of Isaac, and the God of Jacob." The reason of the first injunction was not merely reverence, but it was prompted by the character of Him who spoke. For in the East shoes are worn chiefly as protection from defilement and dust, and hence put off when entering a sanctuary, in order, as it were, not to bring within the pure place defilement from without. But the place where Jehovah manifests Himself — whatever it be — is "holy ground;" and he who would have communication with Him must put aside the defilement that clings to him. In announcing Himself as the God of the fathers, Jehovah now declared the continuity of His former purpose of mercy. His remembrance of Israel, and His speedy fulfilment of the promises given of old. During these centuries of silence He had still been the same, ever mindful of His covenant, and now, just as it might seem that His purpose had wholly failed, the set time had come, when He would publicly manifest Himself as the God of Abraham, Isaac, and Jacob. [7] The same truth was symbolically expressed by the vision of the burning bush. Israel, in its present low and despised state, was like the thorn-bush in the wilderness (comp. Judges ix. 15), burning in the fiery "furnace of Egypt," [8] but "not given over unto death," because Jehovah, the Angel of the Covenant, was "in the midst of the bush" — a God who chastened, but did "not consume." And this vision was intended not only for Moses, but for all times. It symbolises the relationship between God and Israel at all times, and similarly that between Him and His Church. For the circumstances in which the Church is placed, and the purpose of God towards it, continue always the same. But this God, in the midst of the flames of the bush, is also a consuming fire, alike in case of forgetfulness of the covenant on the part of His people, [9] and as "a fire" that "burneth up His enemies round about." [10] This manifestation of God under the symbol of fire, which on comparison will be seen to recur through all Scripture, shall find its fullest accomplishment when the Lord Jesus shall come to judge — "His eyes as a flame of fire, and on His head many crowns." [11] But as for Moses, he "hid his face; for he was afraid to look upon God."

The vision vouchsafed, and the words which accompanied it, prepare us for the further communication which the Lord was pleased to make to His servant. He had heard the cry of His people; He knew their sorrows, and He had come to deliver and bring them into the Land of Promise, "a good land," it is added, "and a large," a land "flowing with milk and honey" — large and fruitful enough to have been at the time the territory of not fewer than six Canaanitish races (ver. 8). Finally, the Lord directed Moses to go to Pharaoh in order to bring His people out of Egypt.

Greater contrast could scarcely be conceived than between the Moses of forty years ago and him who now pleaded to be relieved from this work. If formerly his self-confidence had been such as to take the whole matter into his own hands, his self-diffidence now went the length of utmost reluctance to act, even as only the Lord's messenger and minister. His first and deepest feelings speak themselves in the question, "Who am I, that I should go unto Pharaoh, and that I should bring forth the children of Israel out of Egypt?" (ver. ii). But the remembrance of former inward and outward failure was no longer applicable, for God Himself would now be with him. In token of this he was told, "When thou hast brought forth the people out of Egypt, ye shall serve God upon this mountain." Evidently this "token" appealed to his *faith,* as indeed every "sign" does, whence their misunderstanding by those "who are not of the household of faith" (comp. Matt. xii. 38, 39; Luke xvi. 31). Similarly, long afterwards, a distantly future event — the birth of the Virgin's Son — was to be a sign to the house of Ahaz of the preservation of the royal line of David. [12] Was it then that underneath all else God saw in the heart of Moses a latent want of realising faith, which He would now call forth?

This first difficulty, on the part of Moses, had been set aside. His next was: What he should say in reply to this inquiry of Israel about God: "What is His Name?" (ver. 13). This means, What was he to tell them in answer to their doubts and fears about God's purposes towards them? For, in Scripture, the name is regarded as the manifestation of character or of deepest purpose, whence also a *new name* was generally given *after* some decisive event, which for ever after stamped its character upon a person or place.

In answer to this question, the Lord explained to Moses, and bade him tell Israel, the import of the Name *Jehovah,* by which He had at the first manifested Himself, when entering into covenant with Abraham. [13] It was, "I am that I am" — words betokening His unchangeable nature and faithfulness. The "I am" had sent Moses, and, as if to remove all doubt, he was to add: "the God of your fathers, of Abraham, Isaac, and Jacob." "This," the Lord declares, "is my Name for ever, and this is my memorial to all generations;" in other words, as such He would always prove Himself, and as such He willeth to be known and remembered, not only by Israel, but "to all generations." Here, then, at the very outset, when the covenant with Abraham was transferred to his seed, the promise also, which included all nations in its blessing, was repeated.

In further preparation for his mission, God directed Moses on his arrival in Egypt to "gather" the elders of Israel together, and, taking up the very words of Joseph's prophecy when he died, [14] to announce that the promised time had come, and that God had "surely visited" His people. Israel, he was told, would hearken to his voice; not so Pharaoh, although the original demand upon him was to be only to dismiss the people for a distance of three days' journey into the wilderness. Yet Pharaoh would not yield, "not even by a strong hand" (ver. 19) — that is, even when the strong hand of God would be upon him. But, at the last, the wonder-working power of Jehovah would break the stubborn will of Pharaoh; and when Israel left Egypt it would not be as fugitives, but, as it were, like conquerors laden with the spoil of their enemies.

Thus the prediction clearly intimated that only after a long and severe contest Pharaoh would yield. But would the faith of Israel endure under such a trial? This is probably the meaning of Moses' next question, seemingly strange as put at this stage: "But, behold, they will not believe me, nor hearken unto my voice: for they will say, Jehovah hath not appeared unto thee." [15] To such doubts, whether on the part of Israel, of Pharaoh, or of the Egyptians, a threefold symbolical reply was now furnished, and that not only to silence those who might so object, but also for the encouragement of Moses himself. This reply involved the bestowal of power upon Moses to work miracles. We note that here, *for the first time* in Old Testament history, this power was bestowed upon man, and that the occasion was the first great conflict between the world and the Church. These miracles were intended to act like "a voice" from heaven, bearing direct testimony to the truth of Moses' commission. So we read in Exodus iv. 8 of Israel "hearkening unto" and "believing" "the voice" of the signs, and in Psalm cv. 27 (marginal reading) that Moses and Aaron "shewed the words of His signs among them." But while this was the general purpose of *the three signs* now displayed — first to Moses himself — each had also its special reference: the first to Pharaoh, the second to Israel, and the third to the might of Egypt.

In the *first sign* Moses was bidden to look at the rod in his hand. It was but an ordinary shepherd's staff. At God's command he was to cast it on the ground, when presently it was changed into a serpent, from which Moses fled in terror. Again God commands, and as Moses seized the serpent by the tail, it once more "became a rod in his hand." The meaning of this was plain. Hitherto Moses had wielded the shepherd's crook. At God's command he was to cast it away; his calling was to be changed, and he would have to meet "the serpent" — not only the old enemy, but the might of Pharaoh, of which the serpent was the public and well-known Egyptian emblem. [16] "The serpent was the symbol of royal and divine power on the diadem of every Pharaoh" [17] — the emblem of the land, of its religion, and government. At God's command, Moses next seized this serpent, when it became once more in his hand the staff with which he led his flock — only that now the flock was Israel, and the shepherd's staff the wonderworking "rod of God." [18] In short, the humble shepherd, who would have fled from Pharaoh, should, through Divine strength, overcome all the might of Egypt.

The *second sign* shown to Moses bore direct reference to Israel. The hand which Moses was directed to put in his bosom became covered with leprosy; but the same hand, when a second time he thrust it in, was restored whole. This miraculous power of inflicting and removing a plague, universally admitted to come from God, showed that Moses could inflict and remove the severest judgments of God. But it spoke yet other "words" to the people. Israel, of whom the Lord had said unto Moses, "Carry them in thy bosom," [19] was the leprous hand. But as surely and as readily as it was restored when thrust again into Moses' bosom, so would God bring them forth from the misery and desolateness of their state in Egypt, and restore them to their own land.

The *third sign* given to Moses, in which the water from the Nile when poured upon the ground was to become blood, would not only carry conviction to Israel, but bore special reference to the land of Egypt. The Nile, on which its whole fruitfulness depended, and which the Egyptians worshipped as divine, was to be changed into blood. Egypt and its gods were to be brought low before the absolute power which God would manifest.

These "signs," which could not be gainsayed, were surely sufficient. And yet Moses hesitated. Was he indeed the proper agent for such a work? He possessed not the eloquence whose fire kindles a nation's enthusiasm and whose force sweeps before it all obstacles. And when this objection also was answered by pointing him to the need of direct dependence on Him who could unloose the tongue and open eyes and ears, the secret reluctance of Moses broke forth in the direct request to employ some one else on such a mission. Then it was that "the anger of the Lord was kindled against Moses." Yet in His tender mercy He pitied and helped the weakness of His servant's faith. For this twofold purpose God announced that even then Aaron was on his way to join him, and that he would undertake the part of the work for which Moses felt himself unfit. Aaron would be alike the companion and, so to speak, "the prophet" of Moses. [20] As the prophet delivers the word which he receives, so would Aaron declare the Divine message committed to Moses. "And Moses went." [21]

Two points yet require brief explanation at this stage of our narrative. For, *first,* it would appear that the request which Moses was in the first place charged to address to Pharaoh was only for leave "to go three days' journey into the wilderness," whereas it was intended that Israel should for ever leave the land of Egypt. *Secondly,* a Divine promise was given that Israel should "not go empty," but that God would give the people favour in the sight of the Egyptians, and that every woman should "borrow of her neighbour," so that they would "spoil the Egyptians."

At the outset, we observe the more than dutiful manner in which Israel was directed to act towards Pharaoh. Absolutely speaking, Pharaoh had no right to detain the people in Egypt. Their fathers had *avowedly* come not to settle, but temporarily "to sojourn," [22] and on that understanding they had been received. And now they were not only wrongfully oppressed, but un-righteously detained. But still they were not to steal away secretly, nor yet to attempt to raise the standard of rebellion. Nor was the Divine power with which Moses was armed to be at the first employed either in avenging their past wrongs or in securing their liberty. On the contrary, they were to apply to Pharaoh for permission to undertake even so harmless an expedition as a three days' pilgrimage into the wilderness to sacrifice unto God — a request all the more reasonable, that Israel's sacrifices would, from a religious point of view, have been "an abomination" to the Egyptians, [23] and might have led to disturbances. The same almost excess of regard for Pharaoh prompted that at the first only so moderate a demand should be made upon him. It was infinite condescension to Pharaoh's weakness, on the part of God, not to in-sist from the first upon the immediate and entire dismissal of Israel. Less *could not* have been asked than was demanded of Pharaoh, nor could obedi-ence have been made more easy. Only the most tyrannical determination to crush the rights and convictions of the people, and the most daring defiance of Jehovah, could have prompted him to refuse such a request, and that in face of all the signs and wonders by which the mission of Moses was accred-ited. Thus at the first his submission was to be tried where it was easiest to render it, and where disobedience would be "without excuse."

There might have been some plea for such a man as Pharaoh to refuse at once and wholly to let those go who had so long been his bondsmen; there could be absolutely none for resisting a demand so moderate and supported by such authority. Assuredly such a man was ripe for the judgment of hard-ening, just as, on the other hand, if he had at the first yielded obedience to the Divine will, he would surely have been prepared to receive a further revela-tion of His will, and grace to submit to it. And so God in His mercy always deals with man. "He that is faithful in that which is least, is faithful also in much: and he that is unjust in the least, is unjust also in much." The demands of God are intended to try what is in us. It was so in the case of Adam's obe-dience, of Abraham's sacrifice, and now of Pharaoh; only that in the latter case, as in the promise to spare Sodom if even ten righteous men were found among its wicked inhabitants, the Divine forbearance went to the utmost verge of condescension. The same principle of government also appears in the New Testament, and explains how the Lord often first told of "earthly things," that unbelief in regard to them might convince men of their unfitness to hear of "heavenly things." Thus the young ruler [24] who believed himself desirous of inheriting eternal life, and the scribe who professed readiness to follow Christ, [25] had each only a test of "earthly things" proposed, and yet each failed in it. The lesson is one which may find its application in our own case — for only "then shall we know if we follow on to know the Lord."

The second difficulty about the supposed direction to Israel to "borrow jewels of silver, and jewels of gold, and raiment," and so to "spoil the Egyptians," [26] rests upon a simple misunderstanding of the text. Common sense even would indicate that, under the circumstances in which the children of Israel, at the last, left the land, no Egyptian could have contemplated a temporary loan of jewels, soon to be repaid. But, in truth, the word rendered in our Authorised Version by "borrowing," does not mean a loan, and is not used in that sense in a single passage in which it occurs throughout the Old Testament. It *always* and only means "to ask" or "to request." This "request," or "demand" — as, considering the justice of the case, we should call it — was readily granted by the Egyptians. The terror of Israel had fallen on them, and instead of leaving Egypt as fugitives, they marched out like a triumphant host, carrying with them "the spoil" of their Divinely conquered enemies.

It is of more importance to notice another point. *Moses was the first to bear a Divine commission to others. He was also the first to work miracles.* Miracles present to us the union of the Divine and the human. All miracles pointed forward to the greatest of all miracles, "the mystery of godliness, into which angels desire to look;" the union of the Divine with the human, in its fullest appearance in the Person of the God-Man. Thus in these two aspects of his office, as well as in his mission to redeem Israel from bondage and to sanctify them unto the Lord, Moses was an eminent type of Christ. "Wherefore" let us "consider the Apostle and High Priest of our profession, Christ Jesus; who *was faithful* to Him that appointed Him, as also Moses was faithful in all his house...As a servant, for a testimony of those things which were to be spoken after; but Christ as a Son over His own house; whose house are we, if we hold fast the confidence and the rejoicing of the hope firm unto the end." [27]

[1] Ex. ii. 23. We must ask the reader to read this chapter with the open Bible beside him.

[2] Ex. ii. 23.

[3] Ex. iii. 7; Deut. xxvi. 7.

[4] Palmer's *Desert of the Exodus,* vol. i. p. 117.

[5] This will be shown when describing the ten plagues.

[6] See the illustration and description in Canon Tristram's *Natural History of the Bible,* pp. 391, 392.

[7] Even the expression, "I am the God of thy father," in the singular number, implies the identity of His dealings throughout. All the fathers were but as one father before Him. So closely should we study the wording of Scripture.

[8] Deut. iv. 20.

[9] Deut. iv. 24.

[10] Ps. xcvii. 3.

[11] Rev. xix. 12.

[12] Isa. vii. 10-14.

[13] Gen. xv. 7.

[14] Gen. l. 24.

[15] Ex. iv. 1.

[16] Scripture frequently uses the serpent as a symbol of the power hostile to the kingdom of God, and applies the figure not only to Egypt (as in Ps. lxxiv. 13; Is. li. 9), but also to Babylon (Is. xxvii. 1).

[17] *Speaker's Commentary*, vol. i. p. 265.

[18] Ex. iv. 20.

[19] Numb. xi. 12.

[20] Ex. vii. 1.

[21] Ex. iv. 18.

[22] Gen, xlvii. 4.

[23] Ex. viii. 62.

[24] Matt. xix. 16.

[25] Matt. viii. 19.

[26] Ex. iii. 22.

[27] Heb. iii. 1, 2, 5, 6.

Chapter Five

(Exodus iv. 17-31.)

Scripture-History is full of Seemingly strange contrasts. Unintelligible to the superficial observer, the believing heart rejoices to trace in them, side by side, the difference between what appears to the eye of man and what really is before God; and then between the power of God, and the humbleness of the means and circumstances through which He chooses to manifest it. The object of the one is to draw out our faith, and to encourage it in circumstances which least promise success; that of the other, to give all the glory to God, and ever to direct our eye from earth to heaven. So it was, when, in the days of His flesh, neither Israel nor the Gentiles recognised the royal dignity of Christ in Him who entered Jerusalem, "meek, and riding upon an ass and the colt of an ass." And so it also appeared, when, in the simple language of Scripture, "Moses took his wife and his sons, and set them upon an ass, and he returned to the land of Egypt: and Moses took the rod of God in his hand." [1] What a contrast! He who bears in his hand the rod of God is dismissed in this mean manner — his wife and sons, and all their goods laden on one ass, and himself humbly walking by their side! Who would have recognised in this humble guise him who carried that by which he would smite down the pride of Pharaoh and the might of Egypt?

On his return from "the mount of God," Moses had simply announced to his father-in-law his purpose of revisiting Egypt. Probably Jethro had not sufficient enlightenment for Moses to communicate to him the Divine vision. Besides, the relations between them at the time (as we gather even from the manner in which Jethro allowed him to depart) seem not to have been such as to invite special confidence; possibly, it might have only raised hindrances on the part of Jethro or of Zipporah. But it was an indication that God furthered his way, when alike his father-in-law and his wife so readily agreed to an expedition which, in the circumstances, might have been fraught with great danger. And this was not all. *After he had resolved to go, but before he actually set out,* God encouraged him by the information that all the men were dead who had sought his life. Again, while on his journey. He gave him threefold strengthening for the work before him. First, He pointed him to the Divine rod in his hand, with which he was to attest by miracles his mission to

Pharaoh. [2] Secondly, lest he should be discouraged by the failure of these signs to secure Pharaoh's submission, God not only foretold the hardening of the king's heart, but by saying, "I will harden his heart" (ver. 21), proved that that event also was under His own immediate control and direction. Lastly, in the message which he was to bear to Pharaoh a double assurance was conveyed (vers. 22, 23). Jehovah demanded freedom for the people, because "Israel is my son, even my firstborn," and He threatened, in case of Pharaoh's refusal, "to slay" his "son," even the king's "firstborn." So terrible a threat was to prove the earnestness of the Divine demand and purpose. On the other hand, the title given to Israel implied that God would not leave "His firstborn" in the bondage of Egypt. In the contest with Pharaoh Jehovah would surely prevail. That precious relationship between God and His people, which was fully established in the covenant at Mount Sinai, [3] might be said to have commenced with the call of Abraham. Israel was "the son of God" by election^ by grace, and by adoption. [4] As such, the Lord would never withdraw His love from him, [5] but pity him even as a father his children; [6] and, although He would chastise the people for their sins, yet would He not withdraw His mercy from them. Such a relationship is nowhere else in the Old Testament indicated as subsisting between God and any other nation. But it is exceedingly significant that Israel is only called "the firstborn." For this conveys that Israel was not to be alone in the family of God, but that, in accordance with the promise to Abraham, other sons should be born into the Father's house. Thus even the highest promise spoken to Israel included in it the assurance of future blessing to the Gentiles.

And yet he who was to declare Israel the heir to this precious legacy was himself at the time living in breach of the sign of that very covenant! His own second son [7] had not been circumcised according to the Divine commandment [8] — whether from neglect, owing to faith discouraged, or, more probably, as we gather from the subsequent conduct of Zipporah, on account of his wife's opposition, which in his depressed circumstances he could not overcome. But judgment must begin at the house of God; and no one is fit to be employed as an instrument for God who in any way lives in breach of His commandments. God met even His chosen servant Moses as an enemy. His life was in imminent danger, and Zipporah had to submit, however reluctantly, to the ordinance of God. But her mood and manner showed that as yet she was not prepared to be Moses' helpmate in the work before him. He seems to have understood this, and to have sent her and the children back to his father-in-law. Only at a later period, when he had "heard of all that God had done for Moses and for Israel His people," did Jethro himself bring them again to Moses. [9]

Thus purged from the leaven of sin, Moses continued his journey. Once more God had anticipated His servant's difficulties; we might almost say, the fulfilment of His own promises. Already He had directed Aaron "to go into the wilderness to meet Moses." At the mount of God the two brothers met, and Aaron willingly joined the Divine mission of Moses. Arrived in Egypt, they soon "gathered together all the elders of the children of Israel." At hearing of the gracious tidings which Aaron announced, and at sight of "the signs" with which he attested them, it is said: "they bowed their heads and worshipped." Then God had not forsaken His people whom He foreknew! So then, not Moses' unbelieving fears (iv. 1), but God's gracious promise (iii. 18), had in this respect also been amply realised. Neither their long stay in Egypt nor their bondage had extinguished their faith in the God of their fathers, or their hope of deliverance. However grievously they might afterwards err and sin, the tidings that "Jehovah had visited" His people came not upon them as strange or incredible. More than that, their faith was mingled with humiliation and worship.

Before we pass to an account of the wonders by which Moses was so soon to prove before Pharaoh the reality of his mission, it may be convenient here briefly to consider a very solemn element in the history of these transactions — we mean, the hardening of Pharaoh's heart. Not that we can ever hope fully to understand what touches the councils of God, the administration of His government, the mysterious connection between the creature and the Creator, and the solemn judgments by which He vindicates His power over the rebellious. But a reverent consideration of some points, taken directly from the text itself, may help us at leasts like Israel of old, to "bow our heads and worship." We have already noticed, that before Moses had returned into Egypt, [10] God had declared of Pharaoh, "I will harden his heart," placing this phase in the foreground, that Moses might be assured of God's overruling will in the matter. For a similar purpose, only much more fully expressed, God now again announced to Moses, *before the commencement of the ten plagues,* [11] "I will harden Pharaoh's heart, and multiply My signs and My wonders in the land of Egypt." These are the two first statements about the hardening of Pharaoh's heart. In both cases the agency is ascribed to God; but in both cases the event is yet future, and the announcement is only made in order to explain to Moses what his faith almost needed to know.

Twice ten times in the course of this history does the expression *hardening* occur in connection with Pharaoh. Although in our English version only the word "harden" is used, in the Hebrew original three different terms are employed, of which one (as in Ex. vii. 3) literally means *to make hard* or *insensible,* the other (as in x. i) *to make heavy,* that is, unimpressionable, and the third (as in xiv. 4), *to make firm* or *stiff,* so as to be immovable. Now it is remarkable, that of the twenty passages which speak of Pharaoh's hardening, exactly ten ascribe it to Pharaoh himself, and ten to God, [12] and that in both cases precisely the same three terms are used. Thus the making "hard," "heavy," and "firm" of the heart is exactly as often and in precisely the same terms traced to the agency of Pharaoh himself as to that of God. As a German writer aptly remarks: "The effect of the one is the hardening of man to his own destruction; that of the other, the hardening of man to the glory of God."

Proceeding further, we find that, with the exception of the two passages [13] in which the Divine agency in hardening is beforehand announced to Moses for his instruction, the hardening process is during the course of the actual history, in the first place, traced only to Pharaoh himself. Thus, before the ten plagues, and when Aaron first proved his Divine mission by converting the rod into a serpent, [14] "the heart of Pharaoh was hardened," that is, by himself (vers. 13, 14). [15] Similarly, after each of the first five plagues (vii. 22; viii. 15: viii. 19; viii. 32; ix. 7) the hardening is also expressly attributed to Pharaoh himself Only when still resisting after the sixth plague do we read for the first time, that "the Lord made firm the heart of Pharaoh" (ix. 12). But even so, space for repentance must have been left, for after the seventh plague we read again (ix. 34) that "Pharaoh made heavy his heart;" and it is only after the eighth plague that the agency is exclusively ascribed to God.

Moreover, we have to consider the *progress* of this hardening on the part of Pharaoh, by which at last his sin became ripe for judgment. It was not only that he resisted the demand of Moses, even in view of the miraculous signs by which his mission was attested; but that, step by step, the hand of God became more clearly manifest, till at last he was, by his own confession, "inexcusable." If the first sign of converting the rod into a serpent could in a certain manner be counterfeited by the Egyptian magicians, yet Aaron's rod swallowed up theirs (vii. 12). But after the third plague, the magicians themselves confessed their inability to carry on the contest, declaring: "This is the finger of God" (viii. 19). If any doubt had still been left upon his mind, it must have been removed by the evidence presented after the fifth plague (ix. 7), when "Pharaoh sent, and, behold, there was not one of the cattle of the Israelites dead." Some of the Egyptians, at least, had profited by this lesson, and on the announcement of the seventh plague housed their cattle from the predicted hail and fire (ix. 20, 21). Lastly, after that seventh plague, Pharaoh himself acknowledged his sin and wrong (ix. 27), and promised to let Israel go (ver. 28). Yet after all, on its removal, he once more hardened his heart (ver. 35)! Can we wonder that such high-handed and inexcusable rebeUion should have been ripe for the judgment which appeared in the Divine hardening of his heart? Assuredly in such a contest between the pride and daring of the creature and the might of the Lord God, the truth of this Divine declaration had to be publicly manifested: "Even for this purpose have I raised thee up, that I might show My power in thee, and that My name might be declared throughout all the earth." [16]

For the long-suffering and patience of God will not always wait. It is indeed most true, that "God hath no pleasure in the death of the wicked, but rather that he be converted and live," [17] and that He "will have all men come to the knowledge of the truth and be saved." [18] But "he that being often reproved hardeneth his neck, shall suddenly be destroyed, and that without remedy." [19] The same manifestation of God which to the believing is "a savour of life unto life," is to those who resist it "a savour of death unto death."

As one has written, "the sunlight shining upon our earth produces opposite results according to the nature of the soil." In Scripture language: [20] "the earth which drinketh in the rain that cometh oft upon it, and bringeth forth herbs meet for them by whom it is dressed, receiveth blessing from God: but that which beareth thorns and briars is rejected, and is nigh unto cursing; whose end is to be burned." Or, as a German writer puts it: "It is the curse of sin that it makes the hard heart ever harder against the gracious drawing of the Divine love, patience, and long-suffering." Thus they who harden themselves fall at last under the Divine judgment of hardening, with all the terrible consequences which it involves.

Hitherto we have only traced this as it appears in the course of Pharaoh's history. There are, however, deeper bearings of the question, connected with the Divine dealings, the sovereignty, and the power of God. For such inquiries this is obviously not the place. Suffice it to draw some practical lessons. First and foremost, we learn the insufficiency of even the most astounding miracles to subdue the rebellious will, to change the heart, or to subject a man unto God. Our blessed Lord Himself has said of a somewhat analogous case, that men would not believe even though one rose from the dead. [21] And His statement has been only too amply verified in the history of the world since His own resurrection. Religion is matter of the heart, and no intellectual conviction, without the agency of the Holy Spirit, affects the inmost springs of our lives. Secondly, a more terrible exhibition of the daring of human pride, the confidence of worldly power, and the deceitfulness of sin than that presented by the history of this Pharaoh can scarcely be conceived. And yet the lesson seems to have been overlooked by too many! Not only sacred history but possibly our own experience may furnish instances of similar tendencies; and in the depths of his own soul each believer must have felt his danger in this respect, for "the heart is deceitful above all things, and desperately wicked." Lastly, resistance to God must assuredly end in fearful judgment. Each conviction suppressed, each admonition stifled, each loving offer rejected, tends towards increasing spiritual insensibility, and that in which it ends. It is wisdom and safety to watch for the blessed influences of God's Spirit, and to throw open our hearts to the sunlight of His grace.

[1] Ex. iv. 20.
[2] Ex. iv. 21.
[3] Ex. xix. 5.
[4] Deut. xxxii. 18; Is. lxiv. 8; Jer. iii. 4; Mal. i. 6; ii, 10.
[5] Hos. xi. 1; Jer. xxxi. 9-20.
[6] Ps. ciii. 13.
[7] From Ex. iv. 25, we gather that only one son required to be circumcised. This would, of course, be the younger of the two.
[8] Gen. xvii. 14.
[9] Ex. xviii. 1-7.
[10] Ex. iv. 21.
[11] Ex. vii. 3.
[12] Perhaps we ought to mark that *ten* is the number of completeness. The ten passages in which the hardening is traced to Pharaoh himself are 1 Ex. vii. 13 ("the heart of Pharaoh was firm" or "stiff"); ver. 14 ("was heavy"); ver. 22 ("firm"); viii. 15 ("made heavy"); ver.

41

19 (was "firm"); ver. 32; ix. 7, 34 ("heavy"); ver. 35 ("firm"); xiii. 15 ("Pharaoh made hard," viz., his heart). The ten passages in which it is traced to the agency of God are: Ex. iv. 21; vii. 3; ix. 12; x. 1; x. 20; x. 27; xi. 10; xiv. 4; xiv. 8; xiv. 17.

[13] Ex. iv. 21 and vii. 3.

[14] Ex. vii. 10.

[15] The rendering in our Authorised Version conveys a wrong impression, as if *God* had hardened Pharaoh's heart.

[16] Rom. ix. 17.

[17] Ezek. xxxiii. 11.

[18] I Tim. ii. 4, comp. 2 Pet. iii. 9.

[19] Prov. xxix. 1.

[20] Heb. vi. 7, 8.

[21] Luke xvi. 31.

Chapter Six

(Exodus v.-xii. 30.) [1]

The predicted trial was soon to come. Provoked through the daring of man, who would measure his strength against that of the living God, it was to establish two facts for all ages and to all mankind. In sight of Egypt (Ex. vii. 5) and of Israel (x. 2) it was to evidence that God was Jehovah, the only true and the living God, far above all power of men and of gods. [2] This was one aspect of the judgments which were to burst upon Egypt. [3] The other was, that He was the faithful Covenant-God, who remembered His promises, and would bring out His people "with a stretched-out arm and with great judgments," to take them to Himself for a people, and to be to them a God (vi. 1-8). These are the eternal truths which underlie the history of Israel's deliverance from Egypt. How Israel had understood and taught them to their children, appears from many passages of Scripture, especially from Ps. lxxviii. and cv. Nor is their application less suited to our wants. It exhibits alike the Law and the Gospel — the severity and the goodness of God — and may be summed up in that grand proclamation unto all the world: "Jehovah reigneth." [4]

The sacred narrative here consists of two parts: the one preparatory, so far as all parties in this history are concerned — Pharaoh, Israel, and Moses; the other describing the successive "signs" in which Jehovah manifested Himself and His power, and by which He achieved both the deliverance of Israel and His judgments upon Pharaoh and Egypt. And here we shall notice successive progress: *externally* in the character of the *plagues* sent by God, and *internally* in their effect upon Pharaoh and his people.

Twice, before the plagues laid low the pride of Egypt, Moses and Aaron had to appear before Pharaoh: once with a simple message (v. 1-5), the second time both with a message and a sign to attest their mission (vi. 10-13; vii. 8-13). In this also we mark the Divine condescension and goodness. If at the first interview the king could say: "Who is Jehovah, that I should obey His voice to let Israel go? I know not Jehovah, neither will I let Israel go" (v. 2), it became impossible to urge this plea, when, at the king's challenge, "Shew a miracle for you" (vii. 9), Aaron's rod was changed into a serpent. This proved beyond doubt that Jehovah was God, and that He had commissioned His

42

servants, since they wielded His power. The only question still possible was, whether the gods whom Pharaoh served were equal to the Lord. For this purpose the king summoned his magicians, who imitated, in a certain way, the miracle of Aaron. But even so, the inferiority of their power was proved, when "Aaron's rod swallowed up their rods." This assuredly — even taking their own profession of miracle-working — should have been sufficient to indicate to Pharaoh that "Jehovah, He is God" — had his hardness of heart admitted of such conviction. But as between Moses' and Aaron's first and second interview with Pharaoh important events occurred, it may be well briefly to record them again in their order.

After the first interview, in which Moses and Aaron had simply delivered the Divine command, Pharaoh, who had pleaded ignorance of Jehovah (that is, of His Deity and claims), professed to regard the demand of Moses as a mere pretence to procure a series of holidays for the people. They were "vain words" (v. 9) "to let the people from their works" (ver. 4). As "the people of the land" - that is, the Israelites, the labouring class - were "many." to "make them rest from their burdens" (ver. 5) would inflict great damage upon the king. To prevent their having either time or inclination to listen to such suggestions, the king ordered that, while the old amount of work should continue to be exacted, the straw needful for making the sun-dried bricks (such as we find in the monuments of Egypt) should no longer be supplied. The time requisite for gathering "stubble instead of straw" prevented, of course, their fulfilling their "daily tasks." The punishment then fell upon the Israelitish "officers," or rather "scribes," whom the Egyptian "taskmasters" had set over the work and held responsible for it. An appeal to Pharaoh only explained the cause of his increased severity, and the "officers" of a people which but lately had acknowledged that God had visited them, not seeing that visitation, but rather seemingly the opposite, ventured in their unbelief to appeal to Jehovah against Moses and Aaron! So rapidly do the results of a faith which cometh only by the hearing of the ear give way before discouragements.

As for Moses, the hour of his severest trial had now come. With the words of Israel's complaint he went straight to the Lord, yet, as St. Augustine remarks, not in the language of contumacy or of anger, but of inquiry and prayer. To his question: "Lord, wherefore hast Thou so evil entreated this people?" (v. 22) — as so often to our inquiries into God's "Wherefore" — no reply of any kind was made. "What I do thou knowest not now, but thou shalt know hereafter." To us, indeed, the "need be" of making the yoke of Egypt as galling as possible seems now evident, as we remember how the heart of the people clung to the flesh-pots of Egypt, even after they had tasted the heavenly manna; [5] and the yet higher "need be for it," since the lower Israel's condition and the more tyrannical Pharaoh's oppression, the more glorious the triumph of Jehovah, and the more complete the manifestation of His enemy's impotence. But in Moses it only raised once more, at this season of depression, the question of his fitness for the work which he had undertaken.

For when Satan cannot otherwise oppose, he calls forth in us unbelieving doubts as to our aptitude or call for a work. The direction which Moses now received from God applies, in principle, to all similar cases. It conveyed a fresh assurance that God would certainly accomplish His purpose; it gave a fuller revelation of His character as Jehovah, with the special promises which this implied (vi. 2-8); and it renewed the commission to Moses to undertake the work, accompanied by encouragements and assurances suitable in the circumstances.

One point here claims special attention, not only on account of the difficulties which it presents to the general reader, but also because its lessons are so precious. When, on the occasion just referred to, God said to Moses (Ex. vi. 2, 3): "I am Jehovah: and I appeared unto Abraham, unto Isaac, and unto Jacob in *El Shaddai* (God Almighty), but *as to* My Name *Jehovah* was I not known to them," [6] it cannot, of course, mean, that the patriarchs were ignorant of the special designation *Jehovah,* since it frequently occurs in their history. [7] To understand this passage aright, we must bear in mind the meaning of the expression "name" as applied to God, and that of the term "Jehovah." By the "name of God" we are of course to understand not a mere appellation of God, but that by which He makes Himself known to man. Now Scripture teaches us that we only *know* God in so far as He *manifests,* or reveals Himself. Hence the peculiar *name* of God indicates the peculiar manner in which He had manifested Himself, or, in other words, the character of His dealings at the time. Now the character of God's dealings — and therefore His name — was in patriarchal times unquestionably *El Shaddai* (Gen. xvii. 1; xxxv. 11; xlviii. 3). But His manifestation as Jehovah — the dealings by which, in the sight of all men, He made Himself known as such — belonged not to that, but to a later period. For the term "Jehovah" literally means, "He who is," which agrees with the explanation given by God Himself: "He who is that He is." [8] As here used, the word *"to be"* refers not to the essential nature of God, but to His relationship towards man. In that relationship God manifested Himself, and He was known as Jehovah — as "He who is that He is," in other words, as unchangeable — when, after centuries of silence, and after the condition of Israel in Egypt had become almost hopeless, He showed that He had not forgotten His promise given to the fathers, that He had all along been preparing its fulfilment; and that neither the resistance of Pharaoh nor the might of Egypt could stay His hand. Viewed in this light, the distinction between the original El Shaddai manifestation to the patriarchs and the Jehovah knowledge vouchsafed to the children of Israel becomes both clear and emphatic.

But to return. The first interview of Moses with Pharaoh had served to determine the relationship of all parties in reference to the Divine command. It had brought out the enmity of Pharaoh, ripening for judgment; the unbelief of Israel, needing much discipline; and even the weakness of Moses. There, at the outset of his work, even as the Lord Jesus at the commencement of His ministry he was tempted of the adversary, and overcame by the word of God. Yet how great in this also, is the difference between the type and the Antitype!

Still, though hardly fought, the contest was gained, and Moses and Aaron confronted a second time the king of Egypt. On this occasion Aaron, when challenged by Pharaoh, proved his right to speak in the name of God. He cast down his rod, and it became a serpent, and although "the magicians of Egypt" "did in like manner with their enchantments," the superiority of Aaron appeared when his "rod swallowed up their rods." Without here entering into the general question of magic before the coming of our Lord, or of the power which the devil and his agents may have wielded on earth before our Saviour subdued his might, and led captivity captive, there was really nothing in what the Egyptian magicians did that Eastern jugglers do not profess to this day. To make a serpent stiff and to look like a rod, and then again suddenly to restore it to life, are among the commonest tricks witnessed by travellers. St. Paul mentions the names of Jannes and Jambres as those who "withstood Moses," [9] and his statement is not only confirmed by Jewish tradition, but even referred to by the Roman writer Pliny. Both their names are Egyptian, and one of them occurs in an ancient Egyptian document. In this connection it is also important to notice, that the Hebrew term for "the serpent," into which Aaron's rod was changed, is not that commonly used, but bears a more specific meaning. It is not the same term as that for the serpent (*nachash*) by which Moses was to accredit his mission before his own people, [10] but it indicated the kind of serpent (*tannin*) specially used by Egyptian conjurers, and bore pointed reference to the serpent as the great symbol of Egypt. [11] Hence also the expression "dragon," which is the proper rendering of the word, is frequently in Scripture used to denote Egypt. [12] Accordingly Pharaoh should have understood that, when Aaron's rod swallowed up the others, it pointed to the vanquishment of Egypt, and the executing of judgment "against all the gods of Egypt." [13] Wilfully to shut his eyes to this, and to regard Aaron and Moses as magicians whom his own equalled in power, was to harden his heart, and to call down those terrible plagues which ushered in the final judgment upon Pharaoh and his people.

Before describing in detail the plagues of Egypt, a few general remarks will be helpful to our understanding of the subject.

1. The plagues were *miraculous* — yet not so much in themselves as in the time, the manner, and the measure in which they came upon Egypt. None of them was wholly unknown in Egypt, but had visited the land at some time or other, and in some measure. As so often, the Lord here employed ordinary natural events. The supernaturalness of the plagues consisted in their severity, their successive occurrence, their coming and going at the word of Moses, their partial extent, and the unusual seasons and manner in which they appeared.

2. We mark in them a regular arrangement and steady progress. Properly speaking, they were only nine plagues (3 x 3); the tenth "stroke" [14] being

in reality the commencement of judgment by Jehovah Himself, when He went out "into the midst of Egypt" to slay its firstborn. Of these nine, the first three were in connection with that river and soil which formed the boast of Egypt, and the object of its worship. They extended over the *whole country,* and at the third the magicians confessed: "This is the finger of God." By them the land was laid low in its pride and in its religion. The other six came exclusively upon the Egyptians, as the Lord had said: "I will put a division between My people and thy people," "to the end that thou mayest know that I am Jehovah in the midst of the land." [15] If the first three plagues had shown the impotence of Egypt, the others proved that Jehovah reigned even in the midst of Egypt. Finally, the three last "strokes" were not only far more terrible than any of the others, but intended to make Pharaoh know "that there is none like Me in all the earth." [16] To show that Jehovah, He is God; that He was such in the midst of Egypt; and finally, that there was none like Him in the midst of all the earth — or, that Jehovah was the living and the true God — such was the threefold object of these "strokes."

3. In reference to the duration of these strokes, the interval between them, and the length of time occupied by all, we know that the first plague lasted seven days, [17] and that the killing of the firstborn and the Passover occurred in the night of the fourteenth *Abib* (or *Nisan*), corresponding to about the beginning of April. In reference to the seventh plague (that of the hail), we have this statement to guide us as to its time: [18] "the flax and the barley was smitten: for the barley was in the ear, and the flax was boiled (or in blossom). But the wheat and the rice (or rather the spelt) were not smitten: for they were not grown." This would fix the time as about the end of January or the beginning of February, giving an interval of at least eight weeks between the seventh and the tenth stroke, or, if we might take this as an average, of more than two weeks between each plague. Computed at this rate, the first "stroke" would have fallen in September or October, that is, after the cessation of the annual overflow of the Nile. But this seems unlikely, not only because the red colouring ordinarily appears in the river at the *commencement* of its increase, but because the expressions (vii. 19, 21) seem to imply that the river was then at its rise (and not on the decrease), and especially because just before this the Israelites are represented as gathering "stubble" for their bricks, which must have been immediately after the harvest, or about the end of April. Hence it seems more likely (as most interpreters suppose) that the first "stroke" fell upon Egypt about the middle of June, in which case from the first "plague" an interval of about ten months would have elapsed prior to the slaying of the firstborn. All this time did the Lord deal with Egypt, and Pharaoh was on his trial!

There is, as we have already indicated, a terrible irony about "the plagues" of Egypt, since in the things in which Egypt exalted itself it was laid low. We seem to hear it throughout: "He that sitteth in the heavens shall laugh: the

Lord shall have them in derision." [19] This will appear more clearly as we briefly consider each of the "strokes."

The first "stroke," or "plague." Early in the morning, during the rise of the Nile, Pharaoh goes down to the river to offer unto its waters the customary Divine worship. Probably, he was accompanied by his wise men and magicians. Here he is confronted by Moses with the message of God. On his refusal to listen, Moses smites, as he had threatened, the waters with the rod of God, and the Nile, in all its branches, canals, cisterns, and reservoirs, [20] becomes red, like blood. Such a change of colour in the Nile was by no means uncommon, or Pharaoh would scarcely have quite hardened his heart against the miracle. In ordinary times this appearance of the river arises partly from the red earth, which the swollen waters carry with them, and partly from the presence of small cryptogamic plants and animalcules (infusoria). The supernaturalness of the event lay in its suddenness, in its appearance at the command of Moses, and in the now altered qualities of the water. "The fish that was in the river died" — thus depriving the people of one of the main staples of their food; "and the river stank, and the Egyptians could not drink of the water of the river," thus cutting off" the main supply of their drink. Somehow the magicians, however, contrived to imitate this miracle, probably on some of the water that had been drawn before "the rod" had smitten the river. And so for seven days, throughout the whole land of Egypt, the blood-like, undrinkable water in every household "vessel of wood" or of earthenware, and in the large stone troughs which stood for general use in the corners of streets and on village-roads, bore testimony for Jehovah. And the Egyptians had to dig round about the river, that their drinking-water might be filtered for use. But "Pharaoh turned and went into his house, neither did he set his heart to this also."

The second "stroke" or "plague" — that of the frogs — was also in connection with the river Nile. At the same time it must be remembered that the frog was also connected with the most ancient forms of idolatry in Egypt, so that what was the object of their worship once more became their curse. Here also a natural occurrence, not uncommon in Egypt, rendered Pharaoh's unbelief not impossible. After the annual inundation of the Nile the mud not uncommonly produces thousands of frogs — called by the Arabs to this day by the name corresponding to the term used in the Bible. These frogs "are small, do not leap much, are much like toads, and fill the whole country with their croaking. They are rapidly consumed by the ibis, which thus preserves the land from the stench described in Ex. viii. 14." [21] The supernaturalness of the visitation lay in their extraordinary number and troublesomeness (viii. 3), and in their appearance at the bidding of Moses. The magicians here also succeeded in imitating Moses upon a small scale. But apparently they were wholly unable to remove the plague, and Pharaoh had to ask the intercession of Moses, at the same time promising to let the people go. To give the king yet further proof that "the stroke" was not natural but of God, Moses left

Pharaoh the option of himself fixing what time he pleased for their removal: "Glory over me: when shall I entreat for thee?" (viii. 9) — that is, let *me* not fix a time, but let me yield to *thee* the glory of fixing the exact time for the cessation of the plague. "But when Pharaoh saw that there was respite (literally, enlargement, breathing-space), he made heavy his heart."

The third stroke, as always the third in each of the three series of plagues, *came unannounced* to Pharaoh, and consisted, not exactly of what we call "lice," but rather of a kind of small insects, scarcely visible, but which penetrate everywhere and cause the most intense inconvenience. Sir S. Baker describes this visitation of vermin, which is not uncommon after the rice-harvest, in almost the words of Scripture: "It is as though the very dust were turned into lice." The "plague" came when Aaron, as directed by God, had smitten the dust of the earth with his rod. As twice before the river, so now the fertile soil, which the Egyptians also worshipped, became their curse. In vain the magicians tried to imitate this miracle. Their power was foiled. But, to neutralise the impression, they "said unto Pharaoh, This is the finger of Elohim" (viii. 19) — the result of the power of a God. *He* has done this. Therefore, being in no way due to Moses and Aaron, it cannot confirm their demand. *We* are vanquished, yet not by Moses and Aaron, but by a Divine power equally superior to them and to us. Therefore "Pharaoh's heart was hardened" ("made firm" and insensible).

And now in the second series of plagues commenced the distinction between the Egyptians and Israel, [22] the latter being exempted from "the strokes," to show that it was not "the finger of Elohim merely," but that He was "Jehovah in the midst of the land" of Egypt (viii. 22). For the same reason, Moses and Aaron were not used as instruments in the fourth and fifth plagues. They were simply *announced* to Pharaoh by the messengers of Jehovah, but inflicted by God Himself, to show that they came directly from His hand.

The fourth stroke consisted of swarms of so-called dog-flies, which not only infested the houses, but "corrupted the land" by depositing everywhere their eggs. This "plague" [23] is to this day most troublesome, painful, and even dangerous, as these animals fasten upon every uncovered surface, especially the eyelids and corners of the eyes, and their bites cause severe inflammation. It was announced to Pharaoh, as he went to the river early in the morning (viii. 20), as has been suggested, probably "with a procession, in order to open the solemn festival which was held one hundred and twenty days after the first rise" of the Nile (*i.e.* about the end of October or early in November). Although it wrung from Pharaoh consent for the people to go, yet on its removal, "he hardened his heart at this time also" — perhaps because in this and the next plague he did not see the instrumentality of Moses, and therefore fell back upon the theory of the magicians about "the finger of Elohim."

The *fifth stroke* was a very grievous murrain (not uncommon in Egypt), which has been supposed to have been of the same kind as the "cattle-plague" in our own country, only far more extensive. But although Pharaoh ascertained, by special inquiry, that Israel had been exempted from this plague, his heart was hardened.

The *sixth stroke* was again made to descend by the instrumentality of Moses and Aaron. As the third in the second series, it came without any warning to the king. Moses and Aaron were directed to take "ashes of the furnace" — probably in reference to the great buildings and pyramids in which Egypt took such pride — and to "sprinkle it up towards heaven; and it became a boil breaking forth with blains upon man and upon beast" (ix. 10). Such "burning tumours breaking into pustulous ulcers," but exclusively confined to man, are not uncommon in the valley of the Nile. [24] Even the magicians seem now to have yielded (ver. 11), but the judgment of hardening had already come upon Pharaoh.

The *sixth plague* had struck not the pride only, nor the possessions of the Egyptians, but their persons. But the three which now followed in rapid succession, stroke upon stroke, were far more terrible than any that had preceded, and indeed represented "all" God's "plagues" (ver. 14). They were ushered in by a most solemn warning, unheeded by him who was nigh unto destruction (vers. 15-18). The reason why God did not at once destroy Pharaoh and his people is thus stated by the Lord Himself: [25] "For now if I had stretched forth My hand and smitten thee and thy people with the pestilence, then hadst thou been cut off from the earth. But now in very deed for this cause have I let thee stand (made thee stand, raised thee up), [26] for to show in thee My power (perhaps, to let thee see or experience it — this is the first reason; the second) — and that My Name may be declared throughout all the earth." That this actually was the result we gather from Exodus xv. 14. Nay, the tidings spread not only among the Arabs, but long afterwards among the Greeks and Romans, and finally, through the Gospel, among all nations of the earth.

Only one day for thought and repentance was granted to Pharaoh (ix. 18) before the *seventh stroke* descended. It consisted of such hail as had never been seen in Egypt, mingled with thunder and fiery lightning. The cattle in Egypt are left out to graze from January to April, and such of the Egyptians as gave heed to the warning of Moses withdrew their cattle and servants into shelter, and so escaped the consequences; the rest suffered loss of men and beasts. That some "among the servants of Pharaoh" "feared the word of Jehovah" (ix. 20) affords evidence of the spiritual effect of these "strokes." Indeed Pharaoh himself now owned: "I have sinned this time" (ver. 27). But this very limitation, and the hardening of his heart when the calamity ceased, show that his was only the fear of consequences, and, as Moses had said, "that ye will not yet fear Jehovah Elohim" (ver. 30).

A very decided advance will be marked in connection with the *eighth stroke.* For here Moses and Aaron, on the ground of Pharaoh's former confession of sin, bring this message from God to him: "How long wilt thou refuse to humble thyself before Me?" [27] Similarly, "Pharaoh's servants," warned by previous judgments, now expostulate with the king (x. 7), and he himself seems willing to let the male Israelites go for a short season, provided they left their families and flocks behind. On the other hand, the hardening of Pharaoh's heart has also so far advanced, that, on Moses' refusal to submit to conditions, the king bursts into such daring taunts as (vers. 10, 11): [28] "So be it! Jehovah be with you as I will let go you and your little ones. Look! for evil is before your faces" {i.e. your intentions are evil; or, perhaps, it may be rendered: See to it! for beware, danger is before you). "Not so! Go then, ye men, for that ye are seeking" (the language evidently ironical). And they were driven out from Pharaoh's presence.

And thus it came, that when "Moses stretched forth his rod over the land of Egypt, Jehovah brought an east wind upon the land all that day, and all that night; and when it was morning the east wind brought [29] the locusts." Once more they were natural means which the Lord used. For the plague of locusts was common in Egypt. Even the heathens used to regard this as a special visitation of God. In Scripture it serves as the emblem of the last judgments coming upon our earth. [30] This "plague," so much dreaded at all times, came now slowly, from far-off Arabia, [31] upon the devoured land, more grievous than such visitation had ever been known, and to the utter destruction of every green thing still left in Egypt — Goshen alone being again excepted. Pharaoh felt it, and for the first time not only confessed his sin, but asked forgiveness, and entreated that "this death" might be taken away (x. 16, 17). Not for want of knowledge, then, did Pharaoh harden himself after that. Yet now also it was not repentance, but desire for removal of "this death," that had influenced Pharaoh. No sooner had his request been granted, than his rebellion returned.

Once more unannounced came the *ninth stroke,* more terrible than any that had preceded. A thick darkness covered the whole land, except Goshen. There was this peculiar phenomenon about it, that, not only were the people unable to see each other, but "neither rose any from his place for three days." It was literally, as Scripture has it, a "darkness which might be felt" — the darkness of a great sand-storm, such as the *Chamsin* or south-west wind sometimes brings in early spring, only far more severe, intense, and long. Let us try to realise the scene. Suddenly and without warning would the *Chamsin* rise. The air, charged with electricity, draws up the fine dust and the coarser particles of sand till the light of the sun is hid, the heavens are covered as with a thick veil, and darkness deepens into such night that even artificial light is of no avail. And the floating dust and sand enter every apartment, pervade every pore, find their way even through closed windows and doors. Men and beasts make for any kind of shelter, seek refuge in cellars and out-of-the-way places from the terrible plague. And so, in utter darkness and suffering, three weary nights and long days pass, no one venturing to stir from his hiding. Once more, Pharaoh now summoned Moses. This time he would let all the people go, if only they would leave their flocks behind as pledge of their return. And when Moses refused the condition, the king "said unto him, Get thee from me, take heed to thyself; see my face no more; for in that day thou seest my face thou shalt die" (x. 28). It was a challenge which sounded not strange in Moses' ears, for before this interview God had informed him what would happen, [32] and directed that Israel should prepare to leave. And Moses now took up the king's challenge, and foretold how after those terrible three days' darkness "at midnight," Jehovah Himself would "go out into the midst of Egypt," and smite every firstborn of man and beast. Then would rise through the night a great lament all over the land, from the chamber of the palace, where Pharaoh's only son [33] lay a-dying, to that of the hut where the lowliest maidservant watched the ebbing tide of her child's life.

But in Goshen all these three days was light and festive joy. For while thick darkness lay upon Egypt, the children of Israel, as directed by God, had already on the tenth of the month — four days before the great night of woe — selected their Paschal lambs, and were in waiting for their deliverance. And alike the darkness and the light were of Jehovah — the one symbolical of His judgments, the other of His favour.

[1] The understanding of this chapter especially will be greatly enhanced by comparing, it throughout with the Bible-text. The object has been not only to tell the history, but, so far as might be within our limits, to explain the statements of Scripture.

[2] Ex. ix. 14.

[3] Rom. ix. 17.

[4] Ps. xcix. 1.

[5] Numb. xi.

[6] Such is the literal rendering, -which in part may remove some of the difficulties.

[7] This view is, however, entertained by some — notably by Josephus, who holds that the name Jehovah was first revealed to Moses.

[8] Ex. iii. 14.

[9] 2 Tim. iii. 8.

[10] Ex. iv. 3, 4.

[11] "It occurs in the Egyptian ritual, c. 163, nearly in the same form, 'Tanem,' as a synonym of the monster serpent which represents the principle of antagonism to light and life." — Speaker's Commentary, vol. i, p. 276, note 10.

[12] Ps. lxxiv. 13; Is. xxvii. I; li. 9; Ezek. xxix. 3; xxxii. 2.

[13] Ex. xii. 12.

[14] This is the literal meaning of the word rendered "plague," Ex. xi. 1. Philo, however, and most interpreters, speak of ten plagues, and regard that number as symbolical of completeness.

[15] Ex. viii. 22, 23. So literally, and not "earth."

[16] Ex. ix. 14.

[17] Ex. vii. 25.

[18] Ex. ix. 31, 32.

[19] Ps. ii. 4.

[20] This is the correct rendering of the expressions in Ex. vii. 19.

[21] Speaker's Commentary, vol. i. p. 279, note.

[22] The word does not properly mean "division" (as in our Authorised Version, viii. 23), but, in the first place, deliverance, salvation, and also separation, distinction, and selection. Thus the Hebrew term, as the reality connects the two ideas of salvation and separation.

[23] Comp. Ps. lxxviii. 45.

[24] A modern writer has supposed them to have been the black-looking, foul ulcers symbolized by the black, rusty ashes of the furnaces.

[25] Ex. ix. 15, 16. We give the correct rendering of the passage.

[26] Rom. lx. 17.

[27] Ex. x. 3.

[28] We give the literal translations.

[29] Or "carried." The storm literally carries the swarm of locusts.

[30] Rev. ix. 3-10.

[31] Generally, it is not the east but the south wind that brings the locusts, from Ethiopia or Lybia. It was purposely from a long distance that they were sent, to show that Jehovah reigned everywhere.

[32] The three first verses of Ex. xi. must have been spoken to Moses *before* his last interview with Pharaoh. Verse 1 should be rendered: "And Jehovah had said unto Moses," etc. They are inserted after x. 29, because they account for and explain the confident reply with which Moses met the challenge of Pharaoh, Evidently, xi. 4, and what follows, form part of that reply of Moses to Pharaoh which begins in x. 29.

[33] If, as we have argued in this volume, the monarch under whom the Exodus took place was Thothmes II., it is remarkable that he left no son, but was succeeded by his widow; so that in that night Pharaoh's only son was slain with the firstborn of Egypt.

Chapter Seven

(Exodus xii.-xv. 21.)

Every ordinance had been given to Israel about the Paschal feast, [1] and observed by them. On the tenth day of the month *Abib* (the month of ears, so called, because in it the ears of wheat first appear), or, as it was afterwards called, Nisan, [2] the "Passover" sacrifice was chosen by each household.

This was four days before the "Passover" actually took place — most probably in remembrance of the prediction to Abraham, [3] that "in the fourth generation" the children of Israel should come again to the land of Canaan. The sacrifice might be a lamb or a kid of goats, [4] but it must be "without blemish, a male of the first year." Each lamb or kid should be just sufficient for the sacrificial meal of a company, so that if a family were too small, it should join with another. [5] The sacrifice was offered "between the evenings" by each head of the company, the blood caught in a basin, and some of it "struck" "on the two side-posts and the upper door-post of the houses" by means of "a branch of hyssop." The latter is not the hyssop with which we are familiar, but most probably the *caper,* which grows abundantly in Egypt, in the desert of Sinai, and in Palestine. In ancient times this plant was regarded as possessing cleansing properties. The direction, to sprinkle the entrance, meant that the blood was to be applied to the house itself, that is, to make atonement for it, and in a sense to convert it into an altar. Seeing this blood, Jehovah, when He passed through to smite the Egyptians, would "pass over the door," so that it would "not be granted [6] the destroyer to come in" unto their dwellings. [7] Thus the term "Passover," or *Pascha,* literally expresses the meaning and object of the ordinance.

While all around the destroyer laid waste every Egyptian household, each company within the blood-sprinkled houses of Israel was engaged in the sacrificial meal. This consisted of the Paschal lamb, and "unleavened bread with," or rather "upon, bitter herbs," as if in that solemn hour of judgment and deliverance they were to have set before them as their proper meal the symbol of all the bitterness of Egypt, and upon it the sacrificial lamb and unleavened bread to sweeten and to make of it a festive supper. For everything here was full of deepest meaning. The sacrificial lamb, whose sprinkled blood protected Israel, pointed to Him whose precious blood is the only safety of God's people; the hyssop (as in the cleansing of the leper, and of those polluted by death, and in Psalm li. 7) was the symbol of purification; and the unleavened bread that "of sincerity and truth," in the removal of the "old leaven" which, as the symbol of corruption, pointed to "the leaven of malice and wickedness." [8] More than that, the spiritual teaching extended even to details. The lamb was to be "roast," neither eaten "raw," or rather not properly cooked (as in the haste of leaving), nor yet "sodden with water" — the latter because nothing of it was to pass into the water, nor the water to mingle with it, the lamb and the lamb alone being the food of the sacrificial company. For a similar reason it was to be roasted and served up whole — complete, without break or division, not a bone of it being broken, [9] just as not even a bone was broken of Him who died for us on the cross. [10] And this undividedness of the Lamb pointed not only to the entire surrender of the Lord Jesus, but also to our undivided union and communion in and with Him. [11] So also none of this lamb was to be kept for another meal, but that which had not been used must be burnt. Lastly, those who gathered around this meal were not only all Israelites, but must all profess their faith in the coming deliverance; since they were to sit down to it with loins girded, with shoes on their feet and a staff in their hand, as it were, awaiting the signal of their redemption, and in readiness for departing from Egypt.

A nobler spectacle of a people's faith can scarcely be conceived than when, on receiving these ordinances, "the people bowed the head and worshipped" (xii. 27). [12] Any attempt at description either of Israel's attitude or of the scenes witnessed when the Lord, passing through the land "about midnight," smote each firstborn from the only son of Pharaoh to the child of the maidservant and the captive, and even the firstborn of beasts, would only weaken the impression of the majestic silence of Scripture. Such things cannot be described — at least otherwise than by comparison with what is yet to follow. Suffice then, that it was a fit emblem of another "midnight," when the cry shall be heard: "Behold, the Bridegroom cometh." [13] In that midnight hour did Jehovah execute "judgment against all the gods of Egypt," [14] showing, as Calvin rightly remarks, how vain and false had been the worship of those who were now so powerless to help. That was also the night of Israel's birth as a nation: of their creation and adoption as the people of God. [15] Hence the very order of the year was now changed. The month of the Passover

(*Abib*) became henceforth the first of the year. [16] The Paschal supper was made a perpetual institution, with such new rules as to its future observance as would suit the people when settled in the land; [17] and its observance was to be followed by a "feast of unleavened bread," lasting for seven days, when all leaven should be purged out of their households. [18] Finally, the fact that God had so set Israel apart in the Paschal night and redeemed them to Himself, was perpetuated in the injunction to "sanctify" unto the Lord "all the firstborn both of man and of beast." [19]

When at last this "stroke" descended upon Egypt, Pharaoh hastily called for Moses and Aaron. In that night of terror he dismissed the people unconditionally, only asking that, instead of the curse, a "blessing" might be left behind (xii. 32). "And the Egyptians were urgent upon the people that they might send them out of the land in haste, for they said. We be all dead men." Ere the morning had broken, the children of Israel were on their march from Rameses, around which most of them had probably been congregated. Their "army" consisted in round numbers [20] of "600,000 on foot — men, beside children" (xii. 37), or, as we may compute it, with women and children, about two millions. This represents a by no means incredible increase during the four hundred and thirty years that had elapsed since their settlement in Egypt, [21] even irrespective of the fact that, as Abraham had had three hundred and eighteen "trained servants born in his own house," [22] and therefore afterwards circumcised (Gen. xvii. 13), whom he could arm against the invaders of Sodom, so the sons of Jacob must have brought many with them who were afterwards incorporated in the nation. With these two millions of Israelites also went up a mixed multitude of varied descent, drawn in the wake of God's people by the signs and wonders so lately witnessed — just as a mixed crowd still follows after every great spiritual movement, a source of hindrance rather than of help to it, [23] ever continuing strangers, and at most only fit to act as "hewers of wood and drawers of water." [24] But a precious legacy of faith did Israel bear, when they took with them out of Egypt the bones of Joseph, [25] which all those centuries had waited for the fulfilment of God's promise. As Calvin aptly writes: "In all those times of adversity could the people never have forgotten the promised redemption. For if, in their communings, the oath which Joseph had made their fathers swear had not been remembered, Moses could in no wise have been aware of it."

Such a sight had never been witnessed in the land of Egypt as when the nation, so delivered^ halted for their first night-quarters at *Succoth,* or "booths." The locality of this and the following station, *Etham,* cannot be exactly ascertained; nor is this the place to discuss such questions. Succoth may have been fixed upon as the general rendezvous of the people, while at Etham they had reached "the edge of the wilderness," which divides Egypt from Palestine. The straight road would have brought them shortly into the land of the Philistines, face to face with a warlike race, against which even Egypt could often scarcely stand. Of course they would have contested the advance of Israel. To such test God in His mercy would not expose a people so unprepared for it, as was Israel at that time. Accordingly, they were directed to "turn" southward, and march to "*Pi-hahiroth,* between *Migdol* and the sea," where they were to encamp.

Two events, as we understand it, marked Etham, the second stage of their journey. It was apparently here, at the edge of the wilderness. [26] that first Jehovah "went before" His people "by day in a pillar of cloud, to lead them the way; and by night in a pillar of fire, to give them light, to go by day and night," that is, to enable them at all times to march onward. In Exodus xiii. 17, 18, we read that "God (Elohim) led the people," but now *Jehovah,* as it were, took command (ver. 21), [27] and, by a sensible sign of His Presence, ensured their safety. This pillar was at the same time one "of fire and of the cloud" (xiv. 24), "of light" and "of cloud and darkness" (ver. 20). Ordinarily, by day only the cloud was visible, but by night the fire, which the cloud had enwrapped, shone out. [28] In this cloud Jehovah was visibly present in the "Angel" of the covenant; [29] there the glory of Jehovah appeared (xvi. 10; xl. 34; Numb. xvi. 42); thence He spoke to Moses and to Israel; and this was the *Shechinah,* or visible Presence, which afterwards rested upon the Most Holy Place. And this pledge and symbol of His visible Presence appears once more in the description of the last days — only then "upon every dwelling-place of Mount Zion." [30]

Secondly, it was probably from Etham, as they turned southwards, that tidings were carried to Pharaoh, which made him hope that Israel had, by this sudden backward movement, "entangled" themselves as in a net, and would fall a ready prey to his trained army. [31] Perhaps now also, for the first time, he realised that the people had "fled" (ver. 5) — not merely gone for a few days to offer sacrifice, as they might have done, close by Etham, but left entirely and for ever. The sacred text does not necessarily imply that from Etham to Pi-hahiroth there was only one day's march. Indeed, opinions as to the exact locality of each of the stages to the Red Sea [32] are still divided, though the general route is sufficiently ascertained. While Israel thus pursued their journey, Pharaoh quickly gathered his army, the principal strength of which lay in its "six hundred chosen chariots." Each of these was drawn by two fiery, trained horses, and contained two warriors, one bearing the shield and driving, the other fully armed. A most formidable array it would have been under any circumstances; much more so to an untrained multitude, encumbered with women and children, and dispirited by centuries of slavery to those very Egyptians, the flower of whose army they now saw before them.

It must have been as the rays of the setting sun were glinting upon the war chariots, that the Israelites first descried the approach of Pharaoh's army. It followed in their track, and came approaching them from the north. There was no escape in that direction. Eastward was the sea; to the west and south rose mountains. Flight was impossible; defence seemed madness. Once more the faith of Israel signally failed, and they broke into murmuring against Moses. But the Lord was faithful. What now took place was not only to be the final act of sovereign deliverance by God's arm alone, nor yet merely to serve ever afterwards as a memorial by which Israel's faith might be upheld, but also to teach, by the judgments upon Egypt, that Jehovah was a righteous and holy Judge.

There are times when even prayer seems unbelief, and only to go forward in calm assurance is duty. "Wherefore criest thou unto Me? Speak unto the children of Israel that they go forward." Yet this forward movement was to be made only after Moses had stretched the rod of God over the sea, and the Angel of the Lord gone behind the host, casting the light of the pillar upon Israel's path, while, with the darkness of the cloud, he kept Egypt apart from them. Then blew the "strong east wind all that night," as never it had swept across those waters before. [33] They divided, and formed on each side a wall, between which Israel passed dry-shod. When the host of Egypt reached the seashore, night had probably fallen, and the Israelites were far advanced on the dry bed of the sea. Their position would be seen by the fire from the cloud which threw its light upon the advancing multitude. To follow where they had dared to go, seemed dictated by military honour, and victory within easy reach. Yet, read in the light of what was to follow, it sounds like Divine irony that "the Egyptians pursued and went in after them in the midst of the sea." And so the long night passed. The grey morning light was breaking on the other side of the waters, when a fiercer sun than that about to rise on the horizon cast its glare upon the Egyptians. "Jehovah looked unto" them "through the pillar of fire and of the cloud, and troubled the host of the Egyptians." It was the fire of His Divine Presence, bursting suddenly through the pillar of the cloud, which threw them into confusion and panic. The wheels of their chariots became clogged, the sand beneath them seemed to soften under the fiery glow, and they drave heavily. With that light from the fiery cloudy the conviction flashed upon them that it was Jehovah who fought for Israel and against them. They essayed immediate flight. But already Moses had, at God's command, once more stretched his hand over the sea. In that morning watch, the wind veered round; the waters returned, and Pharaoh, with the flower of his host, sank, buried beneath the waves. Thus, in the language of Scripture, "Jehovah shook off [34] the Egyptians in the midst of the sea." [35]

Incidental confirmations of this grand event are not wanting. Throughout the Old Testament, it is constantly appealed to, and forms, so to speak, the foundation on which God rests His claim upon His people. Local tradition also has preserved its memory. Nor has anything yet been urged to shake our faith in the narrative. Although the exact spot of the passage through the Red Sea is matter of discussion, yet all are agreed that it must have taken place near Suez, and that the conditions are such as to make it quite possible for the host of Israel to have safely crossed during that night. Moreover, it is a curious fact, illustrating the history of Pharaoh's overthrow, that, according to Egyptian documents, seventeen years elapsed after the death of Thothmes II. (whom we regard as the Pharaoh of this narrative) before any Egyptian expedition was undertaken into the Peninsula of Sinai, and 22 years before any attempt was made to recover the power over Syria which Egypt seems to have lost. And thus, also, it was that Israel could safely pursue their march through the wilderness, which had hitherto been subject to the Egyptians.

But Moses and the children of Israel sang on the other side of the sea a song of thanksgiving and triumph, which, repeated every Sabbath in the Temple, [36] when the drink-offering of the festive sacrifice was poured out, reminded Israel that to all time the kingdom was surrounded by the hostile powers of this world; that there must always be a contest between them; and that Jehovah would always Himself interpose to destroy His enemies and to deliver His people. Thus that great event is really not solitary, nor yet its hymn without an echo. For all times it has been a prophecy, a comfort, and a song of anticipated sure victory to the Church. And so at the last, they who stand on the "sea of glass mingled with fire," who have "gotten the victory," and have "the harps of God," "sing the song of Moses, the servant of God, and the song of the Lamb."

[1] Later Jewish ordinances distinguish between the so-called "Egyptian Passover"— that is, as it was enjoined for the first night of its celebration —and the "Permanent Passover," as it was to be observed by Israel after their possession of the Land of Promise. The sacrificial lamb was to be offered "between the evenings" (Ex. xii. 6, marginal rendering), that is, according to Jewish tradition, from the time the sun begins to decline to that of its full setting, say, between 3 and 6 o'clock p.m.

[2] Esther iii. 7; Neh. ii. 1.

[3] Gen. xv. 16.

[4] The Hebrew word means either of the two. See Ex. xii. 5; Deut. xvi. 2.

[5] Later Jewish ordinances fixed the number of a company at a *minimum* of ten, and a *maximum* of twenty, persons.

[6] Such is the literal rendering.

[7] Ex. xii. 23.

[8] I Cor. v. 7. 8.

[9] Ex. xii. 46.

[10] John xix. 33, 36.

[11] I Cor. x. 17.

[12] Not only in faith but in thanksgiving.

[13] Matt. xxv. 6.

[14] Ex. xii. 12.

[15] Isa. xliii. 15.

[16] The later Jews had a twofold computation of the year — the *ecclesiastical year*, which began with the month *Abib*, or Nisan, and by which all the festivals were arranged; and the *civil year*, which began in autumn, in the seventh month of the sacred year. In Egypt the year properly began with the summer equinox, when the Nile commenced to rise.

[17] The arrangement of Ex. xii. should be noted: vers. 1-14 contain the Divine directions to Moses for the observance of the first Passover; vers. 15-20 give instructions for the *future* celebration of the feast, enjoined later (ver. 17), but inserted here in their connection with the history; in vers. 21-27 Moses communicates the will of God to the people; while ver. 28 records the obedience of Israel.

[18] The *Exodus* brought Israel into a new life. Hence, all that was of the old, and sustained it, must be put away (i Cor. v. 8). To have eaten of leaven would have been to deny, as it were, this great fact. The feast of unleavened bread, which followed the Passover-night, lasted seven days, both as commemorative of the creation of Israel, and because the number seven is that of the covenant.

[19] Ex. xiii. 1-7.

[20] "About 600,000 on foot" (comp. Numb. i. 46, iii. 39). "On foot," an expression used of an army; for Israel went out, not as fugitives, but as an army in triumph.

[21] Calculations have again and again been made to show the reasonableness of these numbers; and the question may indeed be considered as settled. Nor must we forget that a special blessing attached to Israel, in fulfilment of the promise, Gen. xlvi. 3.

[22] Gen. xiv. 14.

[23] Numb. xi. 4.

[24] Deut. xxix. 11.

[25] Ex. xiii. 19.

[26] Ex. xiii. 21.

[27] The expression is the more noteworthy, as, both on a monument and in one of the ancient Egyptian documents, the general is compared to "a flame in the darkness," "streaming in advance of his soldiers."

[28] Numb. ix. 15, 16.

[29] Ex. xiv. 19.

[30] Isa. iv. 5.

[31] Ex. xiv. 2-4.

[32] In the Hebrew it is called "the sea of reeds," but in the Greek translation of the LXX, and in the New Testament, "the Red Sea." The name is differently derived either from the *red coral* in its waters, or from *Edom,* which means "red" — as it were, the sea of the red men, or Edomites.

[33] Rev. xv. 2, 3. The following extract from Palmer's *Desert of the Exodus* (vol. i. p. 37) may be interesting: "A strong wind blowing from the east, at the moment of the setting in of the ebb-tide, might so drive back the waters that towards the sea they would be some feet higher than on the shore side. Such a phenomenon is frequently observed in lakes and inland seas; and if there were, as there would very probably be, at the head of the gulf, any inequality in the bed of the sea, or any chain of sand-banks dividing the upper part of the gulf into two basins, that portion might be blown dry, and a path very soon left with water on either side. As the parting of the sea was caused by an east wind, the sudden veering of this wind to the opposite quarter at the moment of the return tide would bring the waters back with unusual rapidity. This seems to have been actually the case, for we find that the waters returned, not with a sudden rush, overwhelming the Egyptians at once, but gradually, and at first, as we might expect, saturating the sand, so that 'it took off their chariot-wheels that they drave them heavily,' In the hurricane and darkness of the night this would naturally cause such a panic and confusion as to seriously retard them in their passage; but, in the meantime, the waters were too surely advancing upon them, and when morning broke ' Israel saw the Egyptians dead upon the sea-shore,' The verse last quoted seems to show conclusively that the wind did veer round to the west, for otherwise, with the east wind still blowing, the corpses of Pharaoh and his host would have been driven away from the Israelites, and thrown upon the opposite shore." Parallel instances are referred to by Dean Stanley (*Sinai and Palestine,* p, 34), notably that

of the bed of the river Rhone being blown dry by a strong north-west wind.

[34] So literally, as in the margin.

[35] Ex. xiv. 27.

[36] Tradition informs us that the "Song of Moses" was sung in sections (one for each Sabbath) in the Temple, at the close of the Sabbath-morning service. The Song of Moses consists of three stanzas (Ex. xv. 2-5, 6-10, and 11-18), of which the first two show the power of Jehovah in the destruction of His enemies, while the third gives thanks for the result, in the calling of Israel to be the kingdom of God, and their possession of the promised inheritance.

The Wanderings in the Wilderness - Chapter Eight

(Exodus xv. 22; xvi.)

With the song of triumph on the other side the sea, the first part of the Book of Exodus ends. Israel has now become a nation. God has made it such by a twofold deliverance. He has, so to speak, "created" it for Himself. It onlyremains that this new-born people of God shall be consecrated to Him at the mount. And the second part of Exodus describes their wilderness-journey to Sinai, and their consecration there unto God. In this also it may serve to us as the pattern of heavenly things on our passage through the wilderness to the mount.

As Israel looked in the morning light across the now quiet sea, into which Jehovah had so lately shaken the pursuers of His people, their past danger must have seemed to them greater than ever. Along that defile, the only practicable road, their enemies had followed them. Assuredly the sea was the only pathway of safety to them, and in that sea they had been baptized unto Moses, and unto Moses' God. And now, as they turned towards the wilderness, there seemed to stand before them, and to extend all along their line of vision, east and north, a low range of bare limestone hills, that bounded the prospect, rising like a wall. Accordingly they called this the wilderness of *Shur,* or of "the wall." [1] This then was the wilderness, fresh, free, and undisputed! But this also was that "great and terrible wilderness," so full of terror, danger, and difficulty, [2] through which they must now pass. Under the shadow of that mass of rocky peaks, along the dry torrent-beds which intersect them, through the unbroken stillness of that scenery, of which grandeur and desolateness are the characteristics, led their way. A befitting road to such a sanctuary as Sinai! But what contrast in all around to the Egypt they had left behind only a few hours! When we think of the desert through which Israel journeyed, we must not picture to ourselves a large, flat, sandy tract, wholly incapable of cultivation. In fact it is in almost every particular quite the contrary. That tract of land which bears the name of the Peninsula of Sinai, extends between the Gulf of Suez on the west, and that of Akaba (or the Persian Gulf) on the east. Its configuration is heart-shaped, the broader part lying towards Palestine, the narrower, or apex, stretching southwards into the sea. It really consists of three distinct portions. The northern, called the

Wilderness of *Tih,* or, "of the Wandering," is pebbly, high table-land, the prevailing colour being that of the grey limestone. Next comes a broad belt of sandstone and yellow sand, the only one in the desert of the Exodus. To the south of it, in the apex of the peninsula, lies the true Sinaitic range. This portion bears the name of the *Tor,* and consists in the north chiefly of red sandstone, and in the centre of red granite and green porphyry. The prevailing character of the scenery is that of an irregular mass of mountains, thrown together in wild confusion. The highest peak rises to about 9000 feet. Between these wind what seem, and really are, torrent-beds, filled, perhaps, for a very short time in winter, but generally quite dry. These are called *Wádies,* and they form the highway through the wilderness. Here and there, where either a living spring rises, or the torrent has left its marks, or where the hand of man is at work, cultivated patches, fair and fruitful, are found; palm-trees spring up, even gardens and fields, and rich pasture ground. But, generally, the rocky mountain-sides are bare of all vegetation, and their bright colouring gives the scenery its peculiar character. The prevailing tints are red and green; but this is varied by what seems a purple, rose, or crimson-coloured stream poured down the mountain side, while, occasionally, the green of the porphyry deepens into black. Over all this, unbroken silence prevails, so that the voice is heard in the pure air at extraordinary distances. Besides the cultivated or fruitful spots already mentioned, and tiny rock-flowers, and aromatic herbs, the vegetation of the wilderness consists chiefly of the caper-plant, the hyssop of the Bible, which springs from the clefts of the rocks and hangs down in gay festoons; the "thorn," a species of acacia; another species of the same tree, the *Shittim*-wood of Scripture, of which the framework of the Tabernacle was made; the white broom, or juniper of Scripture; and the tamarisk, which, at certain seasons of the year, produces the natural manna. This leads us to say, that it were a mistake to suppose that the wilderness offered no means of support to those who inhabited it. Even now it sustains a not inconsiderable population, and there is abundant evidence that, before neglect and ravages had brought it to its present state, it could, and did, support a very much larger number of people. There were always Egyptian colonies engaged in working its large copper, iron, and turquoise mines, and these settlers would have looked well to its springs and cultivated spots. Nor could the Israelites, any more than the modern Bedouin, have had difficulty in supporting, in the desert, their numerous herds and flocks. These would again supply them with milk and cheese, and occasionally with meat. We know from Scripture that, at a later period, the Israelites were ready to buy food and water from the Edomites, [3] and they may have done so from passing caravans as well. Similarly, we gather from such passages as Lev. viii. 2, 26, 31; ix. 4; x. 12; xxiv. 5; Numb. vii. 13, and others, that they must have had a supply of flour, either purchased, or of their own sowing and reaping, during their prolonged stay in certain localities, just as the modern Bedouin still cultivate what soil is fit for it.

Such was the wilderness on which Israel now entered. During the forty years that Moses had tended the flocks of Jethro, its wádies and peaks, its pastures and rocks must have become well known to him. Nor could the Israelites themselves have been quite ignorant of its character, considering the constant connection between Egypt and the desert. We are therefore the more disposed to attach credit to those explorers who have tried to ascertain what may have been the most likely route taken by the children of Israel. This has of late years been made the subject of investigation by scholars thoroughly qualified for the task. Indeed, a special professional survey has been made of the Desert of Sinai. [4] The result is, that most of the stations on the journey of Israel have been ascertained, while, in reference to the rest, great probability attaches to the opinion of the explorers.

The first camping-place was, no doubt, the modern *Ayûn Mûsa* (Wells of Moses), about half an hour from the sea-shore. Even now the care of the foreign consuls has made this a most pleasant green and fresh summer retreat. One of the latest travellers has counted nineteen wells there, and the clumps of palm-trees afford a delightful shade. There is evidence that, at the time of Moses, the district was even more carefully cultivated than now, and its water-supply better attended to. Nor is there any doubt as to the next stage in Israel's wilderness journey. The accounts of travellers quite agree with the narrative of the Bible. Three days' journey over pebbly ground through desert wádies, and at last among bare white and black limestone hills, with nothing to relieve the eye except, in the distance, the "shur," or wall of rocky mountain which gives its name to the desert, would bring the weary, dispirited multitude to the modern *Hawwárah*, the "Marah" of the Bible. Worse than fatigue and depression now oppressed them, for they began to suffer from want of water. For three days they had not come upon any spring, and their own supplies must have been wellnigh exhausted. When arrived at Hawwárah they found indeed a pool, but, as the whole soil is impregnated with nitre, the water was bitter (Marah) and unfit for use. Luther aptly remarks that, when our provision ceases, our faith is wont to come to an end. It was so here. The circumstances seemed indeed hopeless. The spring of Hawwdrah is still considered the worst on the whole road to Sinai, and no means have ever been suggested to make its waters drinkable. But God stilled the murmuring of the people, and met their wants by a miraculous interposition. Moses was shown a tree which he was to cast into the water, and it became sweet. Whether or not it was the thorny shrub which grows so profusely at Hawwárah, is of little importance. The help came directly from heaven, and the lesson was twofold. "There He made for them a statute and an ordinance, and there He proved them." [5] The "statute," or principle, and "the ordinance," or right, was this, that in all seasons of need and seeming impossibility the Lord would send deliverance straight from above, and that Israel might expect this during their wilderness-journey. This "statute" is, for all times, the *principle* of God's guidance, and this "ordinance" the *right* or privilege of our heavenly citizenship. But He also ever "proves" us by this, that the enjoyment of our right and privilege is made to depend upon a constant exercise of faith.

From Hawwárah, or Marah, a short march would bring Israel to a sweet and fertile spot, now known as *Wády Gharandel,* the *Elim* of Scripture, "where were twelve wells of water, and threescore and ten palm-trees; and they encamped there by the waters." This spot was suitable for a more lengthened encampment In point of fact, we find that quite a month passed before their next stage in the wilderness of *Sin.* [6] Even now this valley, watered by a perennial stream, has rich pasturage for cattle, and many shrubs and trees. Here, and in the neighbourhood, the flocks and herds would find good sustenance, and the people rest. Leaving Elim, the character of the scenery changes. Instead of dreary level plains of sand, as hitherto, we are now entering among the mountains, and the bright green of the caper-plant forms a striking contrast to the red sandstone of the rocks. Hitherto the route of Israel had been simply southward, and in pursuing it, they had successively skirted the Tih, and near Ehm a belt of sand. But now the host was to enter on the Sinaitic range itself From Numb. xxxiii. 10, we know that from Elim their journey first brought them again to the shore of the "Sea of Weeds." The road which they would follow would be from Wády Gharandel through the Wády Taiyebeh, in a south-westerly direction. Here the sandstone would again give place to chalk hills and rocks. Where the road descends to the sea (at Rás Abu Zenimeh) it would touch, probably, the most dreary, flat, and desolate place in the whole wilderness. This spot was the next camping-ground of the children of Israel after Elim. From the shore of the Red Sea the next halting-place brought them into the Wilderness of *Sin* itself. [7] That name applies to the whole extensive sandy plain, which runs along the shore of the Red Sea, from the camping-place of Israel to the southern end of the Sinaitic Peninsula. [8] On leaving the Wilderness of Sin, [9] we read of two stations, *Dophkah* and *Alush,* before the Israelites reached *Rephidim.* The Wilderness of Sin, the modern *El Markhá* is a dreary, desolate tract, which obtains its name from a long ridge of white chalk hills. In this inhospitable desert, the provisions which Israel had brought from Egypt, and which had now lasted a month, began to fail. Behind them, just above the range of chalk cliffs, they would see, in the distance, the purple streaks of those granite mountains which form the proper Sinaitic group. To the west lay the sea, and across it, in the dim mist, they could just descry the rich and fertile Egypt, which they had for ever left behind. Once more their unbelief broke forth. True, it was only against Moses that their murmurs rose. But in reality their rebellion was against God. To show this, and thereby "to prove them, whether they would walk in the law of God or no," [10] that is, follow Him implicitly, depending upon, and taking such provision as He sent, and under the conditions that He dispensed it, God would now miraculously supply their wants. Bread and meat would be given them, both directly sent from God, yet both so given that, while unbelief was inexcusable, it should still be possible. To show the more clearly that these dealings were from the Lord, they were bidden "come near before Jehovah," and "behold the glory of Jehovah," as it "appeared in the cloud." [11] That Presence ought to have prevented their murmuring, or rather changed it into prayer and praise. And so it always is, that, before God supplies our wants. He shows us that His presence had been near, and He reveals His glory. That Presence is in itself sufficient; for no good thing shall be wanting to them that trust in Him.

As evening gathered around the camp, the air became darkened. An extraordinary flight of quails, such as at that season of the year passes northward from the warmer regions of the interior, was over the camp. It is a not uncommon occurrence that, when wearied, these birds droop and settle down for rest, so as to be easily clubbed with sticks, and even caught by the hand. The miraculous provision chiefly lay in the extraordinary number, the seasonable arrival, and the peculiar circumstances under which these quails came. But greater wonder yet awaited them on the morrow. While passing through the Wády Gharandel they might have observed that the tamarisk, when pricked by a small insect, exuded drops of white, sweet, honey-like substance, which melted in the sun. This was the natural *manna* (a name perhaps derived from the Egyptian), which, in certain districts, is found from the middle of May to about the end of July. But "can *God* furnish a table in the wilderness?" Can He command the clouds from above, and open the doors of heaven? Can He rain down manna upon them to eat? That would indeed be to give them of the com of heaven! Truly, this were angels' food, the provision, direct from God, "the bread of heaven!" [12] The Lord did this, and far more. As in the evening. He had "caused an east wind to blow in the heavens; and by His power He brought in the south wind; He rained flesh also upon them as dust, and feathered fowls like as the sand of the sea;" so, in the morning, as the dew that had lain rose in white vapour, and was carried towards the blue sky, there lay on the face of the ground "a small round thing, as small as the hoar frost." "It was like coriander seed, white; and the taste of it was like wafers made with honey." [13] The children of Israel said. Manna! What is that? It *was* manna, and yet it was not manna; not the manna which the wilderness produced, and yet in some respects like it; it was the manna from heaven, the bread which God gave them to eat. Thus it recalls our present condition. We are in the wilderness, yet not of the wilderness; our provision is like the wilderness food, yet not the wilderness manna; but, above all, it is sent us directly from God.

Such assuredly must have been the lessons which Israel was, and which we to this day are, called to learn. The very resemblance in some points of the natural with the heaven-sent manna would suggest a truth. But the difference between them was even greater and more patent than their likeness. On this point let there be no mistake. Israel could never have confounded the heaven-sent with the natural manna. The latter is seen in but a few districts of the desert, and only at certain seasons — at most during three months; it is produced by the prick of an insect from the tamarisks; it is not the least like coriander-seed; nor yet capable of being baked or seethed (xvi. 23); and the largest produce for a whole year throughout the Peninsula amounts to about 700 lbs., and would therefore not have sufficed to feed the host of Israel even for one day, far less at all seasons and during all the years of their wanderings! And so, in measure, it is still with the provision of the believer. Even the "daily bread" by which our bodies are sustained, and for which we are taught to pray, is, as it were, manna sent us directly from heaven. Yet our provision looks to superficial observers as in so many respects like the ordinary manna, that they are apt to mistake it, and that even we ourselves in our unbelief too often forget the daily dispensation of our bread from heaven.

There is yet another point in which the miraculous provision of the manna, continued to Israel during all the forty years of their wilderness-journey, resembles what God's provision to us is intended to be. The manna was so dispensed that "he that gathered much had nothing over, and he that gathered little had no lack; they gathered every man according to his eating." [14] For this marks the true purpose of God's giving to us, whichever interpretation of the verse just quoted we adopt: whether we regard it as describing the final result of each man's work, that, however much or little he had gathered, it was found, when measured, just sufficient for his want; or understand it to mean that all threw into a common store what they had gathered, and that each took from it what he needed.

By two other provisions did God sanctify His daily gift.

First, the manna came not on the Sabbath. The labour of the previous day provided sufficient to supply the wants of God's day of holy rest. But on ordinary days the labour of gathering the bread which God sent could not be dispensed with. What was kept from one day to the other only "bred worms and stank" (xvi. 20). Not so on the Lord's day. This also was to be to them "a statute" and an "ordinance" of faith, that is, a principle of God's giving and a rule of their receiving. Secondly, "an omer full of manna" was to be "laid up before Jehovah" in a "golden pot." Along with "Aaron's rod that budded, and the tables of the covenant," it was afterwards placed in the Holiest of all, within the ark of the covenant, overshadowed by "the cherubim of glory." [15]

Thus, alike in the "rain of bread from heaven," in the ordinance of its ingathering, and in the Sabbath law of its sanctified use, did God prove Israel — even as He now proves us: whether we will "walk in His law or no." [16]

[1] Ex. xv. 22.
[2] Deut. viii. 15; xxxii. 10.
[3] Deut. ii. 6.
[4] A regular Ordnance Survey has been made, under the direction of Sir Henry James, R.E., by Capts. Wilson and Palmer, i.e., four noncommissioned officers of the Royal Engineers, the Rev. F. W. Holland, and Messrs. Wyatt and Palmer. The result was published in a splendid folio volume, with maps and photographic illustrations, and an excellent introduction by Canon Williams. [5] Ex. xv. 25.

[6] Ex. xvi. 1.

[7] Numb. xxxiii. 11.

[8] From the Wády Gharandel *two* roads lead to Sinai — the so-called upper and the lower. Each of these has been ably and learnedly represented as that followed by the Children of Israel. After considerable research and consideration, we have arrived at the conclusion that the balance of evidence is decidedly in favour of the lower road, which, accordingly, has been described in the text. This conclusion has also been unanimously adopted by the Scientific Ordnance Survey Expedition, which investigated the question on the spot. It is of importance for the localization of Rephidim.

[9] Numb. xxxiii. 12-14.

[10] Ex. xvi. 4.

[11] Ex. xvi. 9, 10.

[12] Is. lxxviii. 19-27; cv. 40.

[13] Ex. xvi. 31.

[14] Ex. xvi. 18.

[15] Heb. ix. 4.

[16] Ex. xvi. 4.

Chapter Nine

(Exodus xvii. xviii.)

A sweeter spot or grander scenery can scarcely be imagined than *Wády Feiran*. Here we are at last among those Sinaitic mountains which rise in such fantastic shapes and exhibit every variety of colouring. Following the windings of Wády Feiran we come upon a wide fertile plain, seemingly all shut in by mountains. This is *Rephidim,* the battle-field where Israel, fighting under the banner of Jehovah, defeated Amalek. The place is too full of interest to be cursorily passed by.

Just before reaching the plain of Rephidim, the children of Israel would, on their way from the Wilderness of Sin, pass a large, bare, outstanding rock. This, according to an Arab tradition, to which considerable probability attaches, is the rock which Moses smote, and whence the living water gushed. Now we know that, when Israel reached that spot, they must have been suffering from thirst, since, all the way from the Red Sea, these three days, they would not have passed a single spring, while their march in early May through that wilderness must have been peculiarly hot and weary. Again, it is quite certain that they must have passed by that rock, and under its shadow they would in all likelihood halt. For at that moment the valley of Rephidim before them with its living springs was held by Amalek, who, as the modern Bedouin would do in similar circumstances, had gathered around their wells and palms, waiting to attack the enemy as he came up thirsty, weary, and way-worn. Here then probably was the scene of the miracle of the smitten rock. Beyond it lay the battle-field of Rephidim.

Before following the Biblical narrative, let us try to realise the scene. Advancing from the rock just described upon that broad plain, we seem to be in a sort of dreamy paradise, shut in by strange walls of mountains. As the traveller now sees Rephidim, many a winter's storm has carried desolation into it. For this is the region of sudden and terrific storms, when the waters pour in torrents down the granite mountains, and rush with wild roar into the wadies and valleys, carrying with them every living thing and all vegetation, uprooting palms, centuries old, and piling rocks and stones upon each other in desolate grandeur. At present the stillness of the camp at night is often broken by the dismal howl of wolves, which in winter prowl about in search of food, while in the morning the mark of the leopard's foot shows how near danger had been. But in the days of the Exodus Rephidim and its neighbourhood were comparatively inhabited districts. Nothing, however, can have permanently changed the character of the scenery. Quite at the north of the valley are groves of palms, tamarisks and other trees, offering delicious shade. Here the voice of the bulbul is heard, and, sweeter still to the ear of the traveller, the murmur of living water. This beautiful tract, one of the most fertile in the peninsula, extends for miles along the valley. To the north, some 700 feet above the valley, rises a mountain (Jebel Táhúneh), which, not without much probability, is regarded as that on which Moses stood when lifting up to heaven his hand that held the rod, while in the valley itself Israel fought against Amalek. As a sort of background to it we have a huge basin of red rock, gneiss and porphyry, above which a tall mountain-peak towers in the far distance. Turning the other way and looking south, across the battle-field of Rephidim, the majestic Mount Serbal, one of the highest in the Peninsula (6690 feet), bounds the horizon. On either side of it two valleys run down to Rephidim. Between them is a tumbled and chaotic mass of mountains of all colours and shapes. Lastly, far away to the south-east from where Moses stood, he must have descried, through an opening among the hills, the blue range of Sinai.

But before us lies the highland valley of Rephidim itself, nearly 1500 feet above the level of the sea. Here in close proximity, but in striking contrast to sweet groves and a running river, are all around fantastic rocks of gorgeous diversity of colour, white boulders, walls of most lovely pink porphyry, from the clefts of which herbs and flowers spring and wind, and grey and red rocks, over which it literally seems as if a roseate stream had been poured. In this spot was the fate of those who opposed the kingdom of God once and, viewing the event prophetically, for ever decided.

Wonderful things had Israel already experienced. The enemies of Jehovah had been overthrown in the Red Sea; the bitter waters of Marah been healed; and the wants of God's people supplied in the wilderness. But a greater miracle than any of these — at least one more palpable — was now to be witnessed, for the purpose of showing Israel that no situation could be so desperate but Jehovah would prove "a very present help in trouble." That this was intended to be for all time its meaning to Israel, appears from the name *Massah* and *Meribah,* temptation and chiding, given to the place, and from the after references to the event in Deut. vi. 16; Psalms lxxviii. 15; cv. 41, and especially in Psalm cxiv. 8. The admonition (Psalm xcv. 8) "Harden not your heart, as in Meribah, as in the day of Massah in the wilderness, when your fathers tempted Me, proved Me, and saw My work," refers, however, primarily, to a later event, recorded in Numb. xx. 2, and only secondarily to the occurrence at Rephidim. At the same time it is true, that when the children of Israel chode with Moses on account of the want of water in Rephidim, it was virtually a tempting of Jehovah. Judgment did not, however, at that time follow. Once more would God prove Himself, and prove the people. Moses was directed to take with him of the elders of Israel, and in their view to smite the rock in *Horeb* (that is, "dry," "parched"). God would stand there before him — to help and to vindicate His servant. And from the riven side of the parched rock living waters flowed — an emblem this of the "spiritual rock which followed them;" an emblem also to us —for "that Rock was Christ." [1]

It was probably while the advanced part of the host were witnessing the miracle of the Smitten Rock that Amalek fell upon the worn stragglers, "and smote the hindmost, ...even all that were feeble," ...when Israel was "faint and weary." [2] It was a wicked deed, for Israel had in no way provoked the onset, and the Amalekites were, as descendants of Esau, closely related to them. But there is yet deeper meaning attaching both to this contest and to its issue. For, first, we mark the record of God's solemn determination "utterly to put out the remembrance of Amalek from under heaven," [3] and His proclamation of "war of Jehovah with Amalek from generation to generation" (xvii. 16). Secondly, we have in connection with this the prophetic utterance of Balaam to this effect: [4] "Amalek the firstfruits of the heathen" (the beginning of the Gentile power and hostility), "but his latter end even to destruction;" while, lastly, we notice the brief but deeply significant terms in which Scripture accounts for the cowardly attack of Amalek: [5] "he feared not God." The contest of Amalek therefore must have been intended, not so much against Israel simply as a nation, as against Israel in their character as the people of God. It was the first attack of the kingdoms of this world upon the kingdom of God, and as such it is typical of all that have followed.

Strange as it may sound, in such a contest God will not fight for Israel as at the Red Sea. Israel itself must also fight, though success will be granted only so long as their fight is carried on under the banner of God. That banner was the rod which Moses had received, and with which he was to perform miracles. This rod represented the wonder-working Presence of Jehovah with His people as their Shepherd, their Ruler and their Leader. Yet in the fight which Israel waged, it was not enough simply to stretch forth the rod as over the Red Sea. The hand that holds the rod must also be lifted up to heaven — the faith that holds the symbol of God's wonder-working presence must rise up to heaven and draw down in prayer the pledged blessing, to give success to Israel's efforts, and ensure victory to their arms. Thus we understand this history. Moses chose a band to fight against Amalek, placing it under the command of *Hoshea,* a prince of the tribe of Ephraim, [6] whose name, perhaps, from that very event, was changed to *Joshua* (Jehovah is help). In the mean time Moses himself took his position on the top of a hill, with the rod of God in his hand. So long as this rod was held up Israel prevailed, but when

Moses' hands drooped from weariness, Amalek prevailed. Then Aaron and Hur — the latter a descendant of Judah, and the grandfather of Bezaleel, [7] who seems to have held among the laity a position akin to that of Aaron [8] — stayed the hands of Moses until the going down of the sun, and the defeat of Amalek was complete.

This holding up of Moses' hands has been generally regarded as symbolical of prayer. But if that were all, it would be difficult to understand why it was absolutely needful to success that his hands should be always upheld, so that when they drooped, merely from bodily weariness, Amalek should have immediately prevailed. Moreover, it leaves unexplained the holding up of the *rod* towards heaven. In view of this difficulty it has been suggested by a recent commentator, that the object of holding up the hands was not prayer, but the uplifting of the God-given, wonder-working rod, as the banner of God, to which, while it waved above them, and only so long, Israel owed their victory. With this agrees the name of the memorial-altar, which Moses reared to perpetuate the event—*Jehovah-nissi,* "the Lord my banner." But neither does this explanation quite meet the statements of Scripture. Rather would we combine both the views mentioned. The rod which Moses held up was the banner of God — the symbol and the pledge of His presence and working; and he held it up, not over Israel, nor yet over their enemies, but towards heaven in prayer, to bring down that promised help in their actual contest. [9] And so it ever is: Amalek opposes the advance of Israel; Israel must fight, but the victory is God's; Israel holds the rod of almighty power in the hand of faith; but that rod must ever be uplifted toward heaven in present application for the blessing secured by covenant-promise.

If the attack of Amalek represented the hostility of the world to the kingdom of God, the visit of Jethro, which followed Israel's victory, equally symbolised the opposite tendency. For Jethro came not only as Moses' father-in-law to bring back his wife and children — although even this would have expressed his faith in Jehovah and the covenant-people, — but he "rejoiced for all the goodness which Jehovah had done to Israel." More than that, he professed: "Now I know that Jehovah is greater than all gods; for He has shown Himself great in the thing wherein they (the Egyptians) had dealt proudly against them (the Israelites)" (Ex. xviii. 11). As this acknowledgment of God led Jethro to praise Him, so his praise found expression in burnt-offerings and sacrifices, after which Jethro sat down with Moses and Aaron, and the elders of Israel, to the sacrificial meal of fellowship with God and with each other. Thus Jethro may be regarded as a kind of firstfruits unto God from among the Gentiles, and his homage as an anticipating fulfilment of the promise; [10] "And many people shall go and say, Come ye, and let us go up to the mountain of Jehovah, to the house of the God of Jacob; and He will teach us of His ways, and we will walk in His paths."

A very marked advantage was immediately derived from the presence of Jethro. Just as after the conversion of the Gentiles to Christianity, the accumulated learning and research of heathenism were to be employed in the service of the Gospel, so here the experience of Jethro served in the outward arrangements of the people of God. Hitherto every case in dispute between the people had been brought to Moses himself for decision. The consequence was, that Moses was not only in danger of "wearing away," from the heaviness of the work, but the people also (xviii. 18), since the delay which necessarily ensued was most tedious, and might easily have induced them to take justice into their own hands. Now the advice which Jethro offered was to teach the people "ordinances and laws," and to "shew them the way wherein they must walk, and the work they must do." Whatever questions arose to which the ordinances, laws, and directions, so taught them, would find a ready application, were to be considered "small matters," which might be left for decision to subordinate judges, whom Moses should "provide out of all the people — able men, such as fear God, men of truth, hating covetousness" (ver. 21). Whatever came not within range of a mere application of these known laws were "great matters," which Moses should reserve for his own decision, or rather, "bring the causes unto God." And this wise advice was given so modestly, and with such express acknowledgment that it only applied "if God command" him so, that Moses heard in it the gracious direction of God Himself. Nor would it be possible to imagine a more beautiful instance of the help which religion may derive from knowledge and experience, nor yet a more religious submission of this world's wisdom to the service and the will of God, than in the advice which Jethro gave, and the manner in which he expressed it. From Deut. i. 12-18 we learn that Moses carried out the plan in the same spirit in which it was proposed. The election of the judges was made by the people themselves, and their appointment was guided, as well as their work directed, by the fear and the love of the Lord.

[1] I Cor. x. 4.
[2] Deut. xxv. 18.
[3] Ex. xvii. 14.
[4] Numb. xxiv. 20.
[5] Deut. xxv. 18.
[6] Numb. xiii. 8, 16; Deut. xxxii. 44.
[7] I Chron. ii. 18, 19. According to Jewish tradition Hur was the husband of Miriam, Moses' sister. His father Caleb must not be confounded with Caleb, the son of Jephunneh.

[8] Ex. xxiv. 14.
[9] This view seems implied in Ex. xvii. 15, and explains the otherwise obscure words of ver. 16, which we literally render: "And Moses built an altar, and called the name of it Jehovah-nissi; and he said, For the hand upon the throne of Jehovah! War with Amalek from generation to generation!"
[10] Isa. ii. 3.

Chapter Ten

(Ex. xix.-xx. 17.)

It was the third month after leaving Egypt when the children of Israel reached that innermost mountain-group from which the Peninsula of Sinai derives its name. Roughly speaking, the whole district occupies about twice the area of Yorkshire. [1] Running through it, like roads, pass very many wadies, all seemingly leading up to the grand central sanctuary, where God was about to give His law to His people. This mountain district bears in Scripture two distinct names — *Horeb* and *Sinai* — the former applying probably to the whole group, the latter to one special mountain in it. The meaning of the name Horeb is probably "mountain of the dried-up ground," that of Sinai "mountain of the thorn." At present the whole Sinaitic group is known by the designation of *Jebel Músa*. It forms "a huge mountain-block, about two miles in lengthy and one mile in breadth, with a narrow valley on either side, ... and a spacious plain at the north-eastern end." [2] That plain, at present known as *Er Ráhah*, is computed to be capable of accommodating a host of two millions. Right before it rises Jebel Miisa, from which protrudes a lower bluff, visible from all parts of the plain. This is the modern *Rás Sufsáfeh* (Willowhead), and was in all probability the Sinai upon which the Lord came down, and whence He spake "the ten words." In that case the plain of Er Ráhah must have been that on which Israel stood, and the mound in front, on the ascent to Rás Sufsáfeh, the spot where Moses "separated from the elders who had accompanied him so far on his ascent."

On leaving Rephidim the main body of the Israelites would pass through what is known as Wády es Sheikh, a broad open valley, containing tamarisk trees, and "cut right through the granitic wall." As a turn in the road is reached, "the journey lies entirely through granite rocks, the sharp, rugged outlines of which, as well as the increasing height and sombre grey colouring of the mountains, impart much more solemn grandeur to the scenery." A late eloquent traveller [3] thus describes the approach to Sinai: "At each successive advance these cliffs disengaged themselves from the intervening and surrounding hills, and at last they stood out - I should rather say, the columnar mass, which they form, stood out - alone against the sky. On each side the infinite complications of twisted and jagged mountains fell away from it. On each side the sky compassed it round, as though it were alone in the wilderness. And to this great mass we approached through a wide valley, a long-continued plain, which, enclosed as it was between two precipitous mountain ranges of black and yellow granite, and having always at its end this prodigious mountain-block, I could compare to nothing else than the immense avenue through which the approach was made to the great Egyptian temples."

As we try to realise the scene presented at the giving, the Law, we can well understand how "all the people that was in the camp trembled." [4] The vast plain of Er Ráhah, and all the neighbouring valleys and glens, were dotted with the tents of Israel. No more suitable camping-ground could have been found than this, the best-watered neighbourhood in the whole peninsula, where "running streams are found in no less than four of the adjacent valleys." The plain itself is nearly 5000 feet above the level of the sea. Right in front, cut off by intervening valleys from all around, rises the Horeb group

(.its highest point 7363 feet), and from it projects into the valley, like some gigantic altar or pulpit, the lower bluff of Rás Sufsáfeh (6830 feet) — "the nether part of the mount" — that Sinai from which the voice of the living God was heard. In front is the mound on which Moses parted from the elders. So abruptly does Sufsafeh rise, "that you may literally stand under it and touch its base;" and so thoroughly is the mountain range separated from all around, that there could be no difficulty whatever in "setting bounds unto the people round about," to prevent their going up into the mount, or even touching the border of it. [5] Behind Sufsafeh, on some peak or cleft, Moses was forty days with the Lord, and descending into the adjacent valley, he would — as the members of the Ordnance Survey record they had frequently experienced — hear the sound from the camp without being able to see what passed in it.

But now as the people gazed on it, "Mount Sinai was altogether on smoke." [6] That vast isolated mountain-block — two miles in length and one in breadth — seemed all on fire! As "the smoke of a furnace" it rose to heaven, "and the whole mount quaked greatly," and "there were thunders and lightnings," and "the voice of the trumpet exceeding loud." But, more awful than any physical signs, "Jehovah came down upon Mount Sinai," "and Jehovah called Moses to the top of the mount," and God Himself "spake all these words" of the commandments. For three days had the people been preparing by continued sanctification, and now they stood in readiness at the foot of, although shut off from, the mountain. But even so, "when the people saw it, they removed, and stood afar off. And they said unto Moses, Speak thou with us, and we will hear: but let not God speak with us, lest we die." [7]

This outward sanctification of Israel had been preceded by inward and spiritual preparation. As always, the demand and the command of God had been preceded by His promise. For He ever gives what He asks. It is, as St. Augustine beautifully expresses it, "Give what Thou commandest, and command what Thou wilt." Arrived at the foot of Mount Sinai, Moses had gone up to a lower peak, as if to ask the commands of his Lord, and Jehovah had spoken to him from the top of the mountain. He was directed, before the people prepared to receive the Law, to remind them of their gracious deliverance from Egypt, of the judgments of God's hand, and of the mercy and kindness which they had received. For as "on eagle's wings" had Jehovah borne them, God's dealings being compared to the eagle, who spreads his strong pinions under the young birds when they take their first flight, lest, weary or faint, they be dashed on the rocks (comp. Deut. xxxii. ii). Yet all this mercy — Moses was to tell Israel — was but the pledge of far richer grace. For now would the Lord enter into covenant with them. And if Israel obeyed His voice, and kept the covenant, then, in His own words, "Ye shall be to Me a precious possession [8] from among all nations — for Mine is all the earth. And ye shall be unto Me a kingdom of priests and a holy nation." [9]

The promise thus conveyed was both special and universal; and it described alike the character of God's people and their destination. All the earth was God's, not only by right of creation and possession, but as destined yet to own Him its Lord. Herein lay a promise of universal blessing to all mankind. And with this the mission of Israel was closely bound up. But while all the earth was the Lord's, Israel was to be His "precious possession from among all nations," His choice treasure — for this the Hebrew expression implies — or, as St. Paul [10] and St. Peter [11] explain it, "a peculiar people." The manner in which this dignity would appear, is explained by the terms in which Israel is described as "a kingdom of priests and a holy nation." The expression "kingdom of priests" means a kingdom whose citizens are priests, and as such possess royal dignity and power, or, in the language of St. Peter, "a royal priesthood." So far as Israel was concerned, the outward and visible theocracy, which God established among them, was only the *means* by which this end was to be obtained, just as their observing the covenant was the *condition* of it. But the promise itself reached far beyond the Old Covenant, and will only be fulfilled in its completeness when "the Israel of God" — whom already the Lord Jesus, "the First-begotten of the dead and the Prince of the kings of the earth," "hath made kings and priests unto God and His Father" [12] — shall share with Him His glory and sit with Him on His throne. Thus the final object of the royal priesthood of Israel were those nations, from among whom God had chosen His people for a precious possession. Towards them Israel was to act as priests. For, just as the priest is the intermediary between God and man, so Israel was to be the intermediary of the knowledge and salvation of God to all nations. And this their priesthood was to be the foundation of their royalty.

A still more solemn description of Israel, and of us who are called "the Israel of God," is that of "holy nation." As Calvin rightly observes: "This designation was not due to the piety or holiness of the people, but because God distinguished them by peculiar privileges from all others. But this sanctification implies another, viz., that they who are so distinguished by God's grace should cultivate holiness, so that in turn they sanctify God." The Hebrew term for "holy" is generally supposed to mean "separated, set apart." But this is only its secondary signification, derived from the purpose of that which is holy. Its primary meaning is to be *splendid, beautiful, pure,* and *uncontaminated.* God is holy— as the Absolutely Pure, Resplendent, and Glorious One. Hence this is symbolised by the light. God dwelleth in light that is unapproachable; [13] He is "the Father of light, with Whom is no variableness, neither shadow of turning" — light which never can grow dimmer, nor give place to darkness. [14] Christ is the light that shineth in the darkness of our world, "the true light which lighteth every man." [15] And Israel was to be a holy people as dwelling in the light, through its covenant-relationship to God. It was not the selection of Israel from all other nations that made them holy, but the relationship to God into which it brought the people. The call of Israel, their election and selection, were only the *means.* Holiness itself was to be attained through the *covenant,* which provided forgiveness and sanctification, and in which, by the discipline of His law and the guidance of His Holy Arm, Israel was to be led onward and upward. Thus, if God showed the excellence of His name or His glory in creation, [16] the way of His holiness was among Israel. [17]

This detailed consideration of what Moses was charged to say, will help us to understand both the preparations for the covenant, and the solemn manner in which it was inaugurated. When Moses intimated to the people the gracious purpose of God, they declared their readiness to obey what God had spoken. But as the Lord could only enter into covenant with the people through the mediation of Moses, on account of their weakness and sinfulness, He spoke in a thick cloud with His servant before them all, so that they might see and hear, and for ever afterwards believe. As previously indicated, the outward preparations of the people were twofold. First, they underwent certain purifications, symbolical of inward cleansing. Secondly, bounds were set round Sinai, so that none might break through nor touch the mountain. [18] Then, on the third day, [19] Moses led forth the men, and placed them "at the nether part of the mount," "that burned with fire." There God proclaimed His holy and eternal law amidst portentous signs, which indicated that He was great and terrible in His holiness, and a jealous God, though the fire of His wrath and zeal was enwrapt in a dense cloud.

The revelation of God's will, which Israel heard from Mount Sinai, is contained in the ten commandments, or, as they are called in the Hebrew original, "the ten words." [20] These were prefaced by this declaration of what Jehovah was and what He had done: "I am Jehovah thy God, which have brought thee out of the land of Egypt, out of the house of bondage." [21] This (as Calvin says) "to prepare the souls of the people for obedience." The "ten words" were afterwards written on two tables of stone, which were to be kept within the ark of the covenant, "the mercy-seat" being significantly placed over them. [22] It is not easy to say how they were arranged on these two tables, but not improbably the first four "words" with "the Preface" (in ver. 1) may have occupied the first, and the other six commandments the second Table of the Law. [23] But we only know for certain, that "the tables were written on both their sides: on the one side and on the other were they written. And the tables were the work of God, and the writing was the writing of God, graven upon the tables." [24]

Considering more closely these "ten words" "of the covenant," we notice, first, their number: *ten,* as that of completeness. Next, we see that the fifth commandment (to honour our parents) forms a transition from the first to the second table — the first table detailing our duties towards God; the second those towards man. But our duty to our parents is higher than that towards men generally; indeed, in a certain sense is Divine, just as the relationship to an earthly father symbolises that to our Father in heaven. Hence the command is to *honour,* whereas our duty to men only requires us to *love* them. Again, almost all the commands are put in a *negative* form ("thou shalt not"), implying that transgression, not obedience, is natural to us. But "the commandment is exceeding broad," and requires a corresponding right state of mind. Accordingly we find that the law of the ten commandments is summed up in this: "Thou shalt love the Lord thy God with all thy heart, and with all thy soul, and with all thy strength; and thy neighbour as thyself." Lastly, the first five "words" have always some reason or motive attached to them. Not so those of the second table, which are mostly put quite generally, to show that such commands as, not to kill, not to commit adultery, not to steal, not to bear false witness, are intended to apply to all possible cases, and not only to friends or fellow-citizens.

Passing from general considerations to particulars, we find that the *"first word"* not only forbids all idolatry in thought, word, and deed, but enjoins to love, fear, serve, and cleave to the Lord. [25] The *second word* shows the *manner* in which the Lord will be served — more particularly, not under any image or by any outward representation. As Calvin remarks, it condemns "all fictitious worship which men have invented according to their own minds," and not according to the word of God. The *third word* forbids the profaning of the name of Jehovah, in which He has manifested His glory, by using it either for untruth or in vain words, that is, either in false or idle swearing, in cursing, in magic, or such like. The *fourth word*, which implies a previous knowledge of the Sabbath on the part of Israel, enjoins personal, domestic, and public rest from all manner of labour on God's holy day, which is to be spent in His service and for His glory. The *fifth word* directs honour to parents as (in the language of Luther) "the vicars of God," and hence implies similar reverence towards all God's representatives, especially magistrates and rulers. The *Second Table* progresses from outward deed (in the sixth, seventh, and eighth "words") to speech (ninth commandment), and finally to thought and desire. The *sixth, seventh, and eighth words* apply equally to what may injure our own life, chastity, or property, and those of others. The *ninth word* should be literally translated: "Thou shalt not answer against thy neighbour as a false witness" (or "as a witness of falsehood"). Comparing this with the statement in Deut. v. 20, where the expression is "a witness of vanity," we gather that not only all untrue, but all unfounded statements against our neighbour are included in this commandment. Lastly, the *tenth word* sounds the inmost depths of our hearts, and forbids all wrong and inordinate desires in reference to anything that is our neighbour's. [26]

Such law was never given by man; never dreamed of in his highest conceptions. Had man only been able to observe it, assuredly not only life hereafter but happiness and joy here would have come with it. As it was, it brought only knowledge of sin. Yet, for ever blessed be God: "The law was given by Moses, but grace and truth came by Jesus Christ" [27]

[1] According to the Ordnance Survey the triangle of the Sinaitic Peninsula covers an area of 11,600 square miles.

[2] *Desert of the Exodus,* vol. 1. p. 111. The quotations, when not otherwise marked, are all from the same work.

[3] Dean Stanley, in his *Sinai and Palestine,* p. 72.

[4] Ex. xix. 16.

[5] Ex. xix. 12.

[6] Ex. xix. 18.

[7] Ex. xx. 18, 19.

[8] The word is the same as for "choice treasure" (1 Chron. xxix. 3; Eccles. ii, 8). We have translated the whole verse literally.

[9] Ex. xix. 5, 6.

[10] Tit. ii. 14.

[11] I Pet. ii. 9.

[12] Rev. i. 5, 6; v. 10.

[13] Tim. vi. 16.

[14] Jas. i. 17.

[15] John i. 5, 9.

[16] Ps. viii.

[17] Ps. lxxvii. 13; comp. also Ps. civ. with Ps. ciii.

[18] When we read in Ex. xix. 24, 'Met not the priests and the people break through," we are to understand by the former expression not the Aaronic priesthood, which had not yet been instituted, but those who hitherto discharged priestly functions — probably the heads of houses.

[19] According to Jewish tradition this was the day of Pentecost, fifty days after the Passover.

[20] The Decalogue, comp. Ex. xxxiv. 28; Deut. iv. 13.

[21] Ex. xx. 2.

[22] Ex. xxv. 16; xl. 20.

[23] Most likely not the whole of each commandment, but in every case only the actual direction (such as "Thou shalt not steal ") was graven on the tables. This would give in the Hebrew, for the first four commandments, along with the "Preface," seventy-three words, and for the other six commandments thirty-one words. It is well known that the Roman Catholics and the Lutheran Church combine the two first commandments into one, and divide the tenth into two. But for this there is not the shadow of ground or authority, either in the Hebrew text or even in Jewish tradition.

[24] Ex. xxxii. 15, 16. When we read that the law was "received by the ministration of angels" (Acts vii. 53; Gal. iii. 19; Heb. ii. 2), we are not to understand by it that God Himself did not speak all these words, but either to refer it to those "ten thousands" of angels who were His attendants when He spake on Sinai (Deut. xxxiii. 2; Ps. lxviii. 17); or, more probably, to the difference between the Old and the New Testament dispensations. In the former, the Second Person of the Blessed Trinity appeared only in the Angel of the Covenant; in the latter, He became incarnate in the Person of Jesus Christ, the God-Man.

[25] Deut. vi. 5, 13; x. 12, 20.

[26] In Deut. v. 21 two different expressions are used— the "desire" being awakened from without by that which is seen to be beautiful; while the "coveting" springs from within — from the evil inclinations or supposed requirements of him who covets.

[27] John i. 17.

Chapter Eleven

(Ex. xx. 18-xxiv. 12.)

The impression produced upon the people by the phenomena accompanying God's revelation of His law was so deep, that they entreated that any further Divine communication might be made through the mediatorship of Moses. As Peter, when the Divine power of the Lord Jesus suddenly burst upon him, [1] felt that he, a sinful man, could not stand in the presence of his Lord, so were the children of Israel afraid of death, if they continued before God. But such feelings of fear have nothing spiritual in themselves. While Moses acceded to their request, he was careful to explain that the object of all they had witnessed had not been the excitement of fear (Ex. xx. 20), but such searching of heart as might issue, not in slavish apprehension of outward consequences, but in that true fear of God, which would lead to the avoidance of sin.

And now Moses stood once more alone in the "thick darkness, where God was." The ordinances then given him must be regarded as the final preparation for that covenant which was so soon to be ratified. [2] For, as the people of God, Israel must not be like the other nations. Alike in substance and in form, the conditions of their national life, the fundamental principles of their state, and the so-called civil rights and ordinances which were to form the groundwork of society, must be Divine. To use a figure: Israel was God's own possession. Before hallowing and formally setting it apart, God marked it out, and drew the boundary-lines around His property. Such was the object and the meaning of the ordinances, [3] which preceded the formal conclusion of the covenant, recorded in Exodus xxiv. Accordingly the principles and "judgments" (xxi. i), or rather the "rights" and juridical arrangements, on which national life and civil society in Israel were based, were not only infinitely superior to anything known or thought of at the time, but such as to embody the solid and abiding principles of national life for all times. And in truth they underlie all modern legislation, so that the Mosaic ordinances are, and will remain, the grand model on which civil society is constructed. [4]

Without entering into details, we note the general arrangement of these ordinances. They were preceded by a general indication of *the manner in which Israel was to worship God.* [5] As God had spoken to Israel "from heaven," so they were not to make any earthly representation of what was heavenly. On the other hand, as God would "come unto" them — from heaven to earth, and there hold intercourse with them, the altar which was to rise from earth towards heaven was to be simply "an altar of earth" (ver. 24), or if of stones, of such as were in the condition in which they had been found in the earth. Moreover, as the altar indicated that place on earth where God would appear for the purpose of blessing Israel, it was only to be reared where *God* recorded His name, that is, where *He* appointed it. In other words, their worship was to be regulated by His manifestation in grace, and not by their own choice or preferences. For grace lies at the foundation of all praise and prayer. The sacrifices and worship of Israel were not to procure grace; grace had been the originating cause of their worship. And so it ever is. "We love Him, because He first loved us," and the gift of His dear Son to us sinners is free and unconditional on the part of the Father, and makes our return unto Him possible. And because this grace is free, it becomes man all the more to serve

God with holy reverence, which should show itself even in outward demeanour (ver. 2 6).

"The judgments" next communicated to Moses determined, first, *the civil and social position of all in Israel relatively to each other* (Ex. xxi. i-xxiii. 12), and then *their religious position relatively to the Lord* (xxiii. 13-19)."

The Divine legislation *begins,* as assuredly none other ever did, not at the topmost but at the lowest rung of society. It declares in the first place *the personal rights of such individuals as are in a state of dependence* — *male* (xxi. 2-6) and *female slaves* (vers. 7-11). This is done not only with a sacred regard for the rights of the person, but with a delicacy, kindness, and strictness beyond any code ever framed on this subject. If slavery was still tolerated, as a thing existent, its real principle, that of making men chattels and property, was struck at the root, and the institution became, by its safeguards and provisions, quite other from what it has been among any nation, whether ancient or modern.

Then follow "judgments" guarding *life* (vers. 12-14), with crimes against which, the maltreatment and the cursing of parents (vers. 15, 17), and man-stealing (ver. 16), are put on a level. It is the *sanctity of life,* in itself, in its origin, and in its free possession, which is here in question, and the punishment awarded to such crimes is neither intended as warning nor as correction, but strictly as punishment, that is, as retribution.

From the *protection of life* the law passes to that *of the body* against all injuries, whether *by man* (vers. 18-27) or *by beast* (vers. 28-32). The principle here is, so far as possible, *compensation,* coupled with punishment in grave offences.

Next, the safety of *property* is secured. But before entering upon it, the Divine law, Divine also in this, protects also the life of a beast. [6] Property is dealt with under various aspects. First, we have the *theft of cattle* — the most important to guard against among an agricultural people — a different kind of protection being wisely allowed to owners by day and by night (xxii. 1-4). Then, *damage to fields or their produce* is considered (vers. 5, 6). After that, *loss or damage of what had been entrusted* for safe keeping (vers. 7-15), and along with it *loss of honour* (vers. 16, 17) are dealt with.

The statutes which follow (vers. 18-30) are quite different in character from those which had preceded. This appears even from the omission of the "*if,*" by which all the previous ordinances had been introduced. In truth, they do not contemplate, as the others, any possible case, but they state and ordain what must never be allowed to take place. They are beyond the province of ordinary civil legislation, and concern Israel as being specially *the people of God*. As such they express what Jehovah expects from His own people, bound to Him by covenant. And this, perhaps, is the most wonderful part of the legislation, regulating and ordering what no civil rule has ever sought to influence. As before, the series of statutes begins by interdicting what is contrary to the God-consecrated character of the nation. Thus, at the outset all *magic* is exterminated (ver. 18), and with it *all unnatural crimes* (ver. 19), and *idolatrous practices* (ver. 20). In short, as before in worship, so now in life, heathenism, its powers, its vileness, and its corruptions are swept aside. On the other hand, in opposition to all national exclusiveness, the stranger (though not the strange god) is to be kindly welcomed (ver. 21); widows and the fatherless are not to be "humiliated" [7] (vers. 22-24); those in temporary need not to be vexed by usury (vers. 25-27); God as the supreme Lawgiver is not to be reviled, nor yet are those appointed to rule under Him to be cursed (ver. 28); the tribute due to the Lord as King is to be cheerfully given (vers. 29, 30); and the holy dignity of His people not to be profaned even in their daily habits (ver. 31). Again, nothing that is untrue, unloving, or unjust is to be said, done, or attempted (xxiii. 1-3), and that not merely in public dealings, but personal dislike is not to influence conduct. On the contrary, all loving help is to be given even to an enemy in time of need (vers. 4, 5); the poor and persecuted are not to be unjustly dealt with; no bribe is to be taken, "for the gift maketh open eyes blind, and perverteth the causes of the righteous," [8] and the same rule is to apply to the stranger as to Israel (vers. 6-9). Finally in this connection, the seventh year's and the seventh day's rest are referred to, not so much in their religious character as in their bearing upon the poor and the workers (vers. 10-12).

Passing from the statutes fixing the civil and social position of all in Israel to *their religious position relatively to Jehovah,* [9] we have first of all an injunction of the three great annual feasts. Although strictly religious festivals, they are here viewed, primarily, not in their symbolical and typical meaning (which is universal and eternal), but in *their national bearing:* the Paschal feast as that of Israel's deliverance from Egypt, the feast of weeks as that "of harvest, the firstfruit of thy labours," and the feast of tabernacles as that of final "ingathering" (vers. 14-17). Of the three ordinances which now follow (vers. 18-19), the first refers to the Paschal sacrifice (comp. Exodus xii. 15, 20; xiii. 7; xxxiv. 25), and the second to the feast of firstfruits or of weeks. From this it would follow, that the prohibition to "seethe a kid in its mother's milk" (ver. 19) must, at least primarily, have borne some reference to the festivities of the week of tabernacles; perhaps, as the learned Rabbinical commentator Abarbanel suggests, because some such practices were connected with heathen, idolatrous rites at the time of the ingathering of fruits. [10]

The "judgments" which the Lord enjoins upon His people are appropriately followed by *promises* (xxiii. 20-33), in which, as their King and Lord, He undertakes their guidance and protection, and their possession of the land He had assigned to them. First and foremost, assurance is given them of the personal presence of Jehovah in that Angel, in Whom is the Name of the Lord (ver. 20). This was no common angel, however exalted, but a manifestation of Jehovah Himself, prefigurative of, and preparatory to His manifestation in the flesh in the Person of our Lord and Saviour Jesus Christ. For all that is here said of Him is attributed to the Lord Himself in Exodus xiii. 21; while in Exodus

78

xxxiii. 14, 15, He is expressly designated as "the Face" of Jehovah ("My Face" — in the Authorised Version "My presence"). Accordingly, all obedience is to be shown to His guidance, and every contact with idolatry and idolaters avoided. In that case the Lord would fulfil every good and gracious promise to His people, and cause them to possess the land in all its extent.

Such were the terms of the covenant which Jehovah made with Israel in *their national capacity.* When the people had ratified them by acceptance, [11] Moses wrote all down in what was called "the book of the covenant" (xxiv. 7). And now the covenant itself was to be inaugurated by sacrifice, the sprinkling of blood, and the sacrificial meal. This transaction was the most important in the whole history of Israel. By this one sacrifice, never renewed, Israel was formally set apart as the people of God; and it lay at the foundation of all the sacrificial worship which followed. Only *after* it did God institute the Tabernacle, the priesthood, and all its services. Thus this one sacrifice prefigured the one sacrifice of our Lord Jesus Christ for His Church, which is the ground of our access to God and the foundation of all our worship and service. Most significantly, an altar was now built at the foot of Mount Sinai, and surrounded by twelve pillars "according to the twelve tribes of Israel." Ministering youths — for as yet there was no priesthood — offered the burnt, and sacrificed the peace offerings unto Jehovah. Half of the blood of the sacrifices was put into basins, with the other half the altar was sprinkled, thus making reconciliation with God. Then the terms of the covenant were once more read in the hearing of all, and the other half of the blood, by which reconciliation *had* been made, sprinkled on the people with these words: "Behold the blood of the covenant which Jehovah hath made with you upon all these words (or terms)." [12]

As a nation Israel was now reconciled and set apart unto God — both having been accomplished by the "blood of sprinkling." Thereby they became prepared for that fellowship with Him which was symbolised in the sacrificial meal that followed. [13] There God, in pledge of His favour, fed His people upon the sacrifices which He had accepted. The sacrificial meal meant the fellowship of acceptance; its joy was that of the consciousness of this blessed fact. And now Moses and Aaron, and his two sons (the future priests), along with seventy of the elders of Israel, went up into the mount, "and did eat and drink" at that sacrificial meal, in the seen presence of the God of Israel — not indeed under any outward form, [14] but with heaven's own brightness underneath the Shechinah. Thus "to see God, and to eat and drink," was a foretaste and a pledge of the perfect blessedness in beholding Him hereafter. It was also a symbol and a type of what shall be realised when, as the Alleluia of the "great multitude" proclaims the reign of the "Lord God omnipotent," the gladsome, joyous bride of the Lamb now made ready for the marriage, and adorned with bridal garments, hears the welcome sound summoning her to "the marriage supper of the Lamb." [15]

[1] Luke v. 8. | [2] Ex. xxiv.

[3] Ex. xx. 22-xxiii.

[4] Fully to understand the sublime principles of the Mosaic, or rather the Divine Law, they must be examined in detail. This, of course, is impossible in this place.

[5] Ex. xx. 22-26.

[6] Ex. xxi. 33-36.

[7] This, not "afflicted," as in the Authorised Version, is the right translation, the command extending beyond oppression to all unkind treatment.

[8] So verse 8 literally.

[9] Ex. xxiii. 13-19.

[10] From our ignorance of the circumstances, this is perhaps one of the most difficult prohibitions to understand. The learned reader will find every opinion on the subject discussed in *Bocharti Hierozoicon,* vol. i. pp. 634, 635. It is well known that the modern Jews understand it as implying that nothing made of milk is to be cooked or eaten along with any kind of meat, even knives and dishes being changed, and most punctilious precautions taken against any possible intermixture of the two. Most commentators find the reason of the prohibition in the cruelty of seething a kid in its mother's milk. But the meaning must lie deeper.

[11] Ex. xxiv. 3.

[12] Further details are furnished in Heb. ix. 19-22, where also transactions differing in point of time are grouped together, as all forming part of this dedication of the first Covenant by blood. That this is the meaning of the passage appears from Heb. lx. 22. The sprinkling of the book and the people, as afterwards of the Tabernacle and its vessels, was made in the manner described in vet. 19.

[13] Ex. xxiv. 9-11.

[14] Deut. iv. 12, 15.

[15] Rev. xix. 6-9.

Chapter Twelve

(Ex. xxiv. 12.-xxxiii.)

Never assuredly have we stronger proof of the Divine origin of what we call grace, and of the weakness and unprofitableness of human nature, than in the reaction which so often follows seasons of religious privilege. Readers of the New Testament will recall many instances of this in the Gospel-history, and will remember how our Lord, ever and again, at such times took His disciples aside into some desert place for quietness and prayer. But perhaps the saddest instance of how near the great enemy lingers to our seasons of spiritual enjoyment, and how great our danger of giddiness, when standing on such heights, is furnished by the history of Israel, immediately after the solemn covenant had been ratified.

Now that God had set apart His reconciled people unto Himself, it was necessary to have some definite place where He would meet with, and dwell among them, as also to appoint the means by which they should approach Him, and the manner in which He would manifest Himself to them. To reveal all this, as well as to give those "tables of stone," on which the commandments were graven, God now called Moses once more "up into the mount." Accompanied by "Joshua, his minister," he obeyed the Divine behest, leaving the rule of the people to Aaron and Hur. For six days he had to wait, while "the glory of Jehovah abode upon the mount." On the seventh, Moses was

80

summoned within the bright cloud, which, to the children of Israel beneath, seemed "like a devouring fire" — Joshua probably remaining near, but not actually with him. "Forty days and forty nights" "Moses was in the mount," without either eating bread or drinking water. [1] The new revelation which he now received concerned the *Tabernacle* which was to be erected, the *priesthood* which was to serve in it, and the *services* which were to be celebrated. Nay, it extended to every detail of furniture, dress, and observance. And for what was needful for this service, the *free-will offerings* of Israel were to be invited. [2]

We have it upon the highest authority, that, not only in its grand outlines, but in all minutest details, everything was to be made "after the pattern" which God showed to Moses on the mount. [3] And so we also read in Acts vii. 44, and Hebrews viii. 5; ix. 23, teaching us, that Moses was shown by God an actual pattern or model of all that he was to make in and for the sanctuary. This can convey only one meaning. It taught far more than the general truth, that only that approach to God is lawful or acceptable which He has indicated. For, God showed Moses every detail to indicate that every detail had its special meaning, and hence could not be altered in any, even the minutest, particular, without destroying that meaning, and losing that significance which alone made it of importance. Nothing here was intended as a mere ornament or ceremony; all was *symbol* and *type*. As symbol, it indicated a present truth; as type, it pointed forward (a prophecy by deed) to future spiritual realities, while, at the same time, it already conveyed to the worshipper the firstfruits, and the earnest of their final accomplishment in "the fulness of time." We repeat, everything here had a spiritual meaning — the material of which the ark, the dresses of the priesthood, and all else was made; colours, measurements, numbers, vessels, dresses, services, and the priesthood itself — and all proclaimed the same spiritual truth, and pointed forward to the same spiritual reality, viz., God in Christ in the midst of His Church. The Tabernacle was "the tent of meeting" (*Ohel Mocd*) where God held intercourse with His people, and whence He dispensed blessing unto them. The priesthood, culminating in the high-priest, was the God-appointed mediatorial agency through which God was approached and by which He bestowed His gifts; the sacrifices were the means of such approach to God, and either intended to restore fellowship with God when it had been dimmed or interrupted, or else to express and manifest that fellowship. But alike the priesthood, the sacrifices, and the altar pointed to the Person and the work of the Lord Jesus Christ. So far as the Tabernacle itself was concerned, the court with the altar of burnt-offering was the place by which Israel *approached* God; the Holy Place that in which they held communion with God; and the Most Holy Place that in which the Lord Himself visibly dwelt among them in the Shechinah, as the covenant-God, His Presence resting on the mercy-seat which covered the Ark.

It is most instructive to mark the *order* in which the various ordinances about the Tabernacle and its furniture were given to Moses. First, we have the directions about the *Ark,* as the most holy thing in the Most Holy Place; [4] then, similarly, those about the *table of shewbread* and the *golden candlestick* (xxv. 23-40), not only as belonging to the furniture of the Holy Place, but because spiritually the truths which they symbolized — life and light in the Lord — were the outcome of God's Presence between the cherubim. After that, the dwelling itself is described, and the position in it of Ark, table, and candlestick. [5] Then only comes the *altar of burnt-offering,* with the court that was to surround the sanctuary (xxvii. 1-19). We now enter, as it were, upon a different section, *that of ministry.* Here directions are first given about *the burning of the lamps* on the seven-branched candlestick (xxvii. 20, 21); after which we have the institution of, and all connected with, *the priesthood.* [6] The last, because the highest, point in the ministry is that about the *altar of incense* and its service (xxx. 1-10). This symbolized *prayer,* and hence could only come in after the institution of the mediatorial priesthood. Thus far it will be noticed, that the arrangement is always *from within outwards* — from the Most Holy Place to the court of the worshippers, symbolizing once more that all proceeds from Him Who is the God of grace, Who, as already quoted in the language of St. Augustine, "gives what He commands," [7] and that the highest of all service, to which everything else is subservient, or rather to which it stands related as the means towards the end, is that of fellowship in prayer — the worshipful beholding of God.

These directions are followed by some others strictly connected with the character of Israel as the people of God. Israel is His firstborn among the nations, [8] and, as such, must be redeemed, like the firstborn son of a family, [9] to indicate, on the one hand, that the people are really His own property, and that the life entrusted to them belongeth to Him; and, on the other hand, to express that, in the firstborn, all the family is hallowed to God. [10] This was the import of the "*atonement money.*" [11] But even so, each approach to Him needed special *washing* — hence the *laver* (xxx. 17-21). Again, within Israel, the priests were to be the sacred representatives of the people. As such, they, and all connected with their service, must be *anointed* with a peculiar oil, symbolical of the Holy Spirit, all counterfeit of which was to be visited with such punishment as reminds us of that following upon the sin against the Holy Ghost (vers. 22-33). Lastly, the *material* for the highest symbolical service, that of *incensing,* is described (vers. 34-38). The whole section closes by designating the persons whom the Lord had raised up for doing all the work connected with the preparation of His Sanctuary. [12]

The institutions thus made were, in reality, the outcome and the consequences of the covenant which the Lord had made with Israel. As "*a sign*" of this covenant between Jehovah and the children of Israel, [13] God now ordered anew the *observance of the Sabbath* (xxxi. 12-17) — its twofold provision of rest and of sanctification (ver. 15) being expressive of the civil and the religious aspects of that covenant, and of their marvellous combination. Thus furnished with all needful directions, Moses finally received, at the Hand of the Lord, the "two tables of testimony," "written with the finger of God" (ver. 18).

While these sacred transactions were taking place on the mount, a far different scene was enacted below in the camp of Israel. Without attempting the foolish and wrongful task of palliating the sin of making the Golden Calf, [14] it is right that the matter should be placed in its true light. The prolonged absence of Moses had awakened peculiar fears in the people. They had seen him pass more than a month ago into the luminous cloud that covered the mount. "And the sight of the glory of Jehovah was like a devouring fire on the top of the mount in the eyes of the children of Israel." [15] What more natural than for those who waited, week after week, in unexplained solitude, within sight of this fire, to imagine that Moses had been devoured by it? Their leader was gone, and the visible symbol of Jehovah was high up on the mountain top, like "a devouring fire." They must have another leader; that would be Aaron. But they must also have another symbol of the Divine Presence. One only occurred to their carnal minds, besides that which had hitherto preceded them. It was the Egyptian Apis, who, under the form of a calf, represented the powers of nature. To his worship they had always been accustomed; indeed, its principal seat was the immediate neighbourhood of the district in Egypt where, for centuries, they and their fathers had been settled. Probably, this also was the form under which many of them had, in former days, tried, in a perverted manner, to serve their ancestral God, combining the traditions of the patriarchs with the corruptions around them (compare Joshua xxiv. 14; Ezekiel xx. 8; xxiii. 3, 8). It is quite evident that Israel did not mean to forsake Jehovah, but only to serve Him under the symbol of Apis. This appears from the statement of the people themselves on seeing the Golden Calf: [16] "This is thy God," [17] and from the proclamation of Aaron (xxxii. 5): "To-morrow is a feast to Jehovah." Their great sin consisted in not realizing the Presence of an unseen God, while the fears of their unbelief led them back to their former idolatrous practices, unmindful that this involved a breach of the second of those commandments so lately proclaimed in their hearing, and of the whole covenant which had so solemnly been ratified. Some expositors have sought to extenuate the guilt of Aaron by supposing that, in asking for their golden ornaments to make "the calf," he had hoped to enlist their vanity and covetousness, and so to turn them from their sinful purpose. The text, however, affords no warrant for this hypothesis. It is true that Aaron was, at the time, not yet in the priesthood, and also that his proclamation of "a feast to Jehovah" may have been intended to bring it out distinctly, that the name of Jehovah was still, as before, acknowledged by Israel. But his culpable weakness — to say the least of it — only adds to his share in the people's sin. Indeed, this appears from Aaron's later confession to Moses, [18] than which nothing more humiliating is recorded, even throughout this sad story. Perhaps, however, it was well that, before his appointment to the priesthood, Aaron, and all after him, should have had this evidence of natural unfitness and unworthiness, that so it might appear more clearly that the character of all was typical, and in no way connected with the worthiness of Aaron or of his house.

While Israel indulged in the camp in the usual licentious dances and orgies which accompanied such heathen festivals, yet another trial awaited Moses. It had been God Himself Who informed Moses of the "quick" apostasy of His people (xxxii. 7, 8), accompanying the announcement by these words: "Now therefore let Me alone, that My wrath may wax hot against them, and that I may consume them: and I will make of thee a great nation" (ver. 10). One of the fathers has already noticed, that the Divine words, "Now therefore let Me alone," seemed to imply a call to Moses to exercise his office as intercessor for his people. Moreover, it has also been remarked, that the offer to make of Moses a nation even greater than Israel, [19] was, in a sense, a real temptation, or rather a trial of Moses' singleness of purpose and faithfulness to his mission. We know how entirely Moses stood this trial, and how earnestly, perseveringly, and successfully he pleaded for Israel with .the Lord (vers. 11-14). But one point has not been sufficiently noticed by commentators. When, in announcing the apostasy of Israel, God spake of them not as His own but as Moses' people — "thy people, whom thou broughtest out of the land of Egypt" (ver. 7) — He at the same time furnished Moses with the right plea in his intercession, and also indicated the need of that severe punishment which was afterwards executed, lest Moses might, by weak indulgence, be involved in complicity with Israel's sin. The latter point is easily understood. As for the other, we see how Moses, in his intercession, pleaded the argument with which God had furnished him. Most earnestly did -he insist that Israel was *God's* people, since their deliverance from Egypt had been wholly God-wrought. Three special arguments did he use with God, and *these three may to all time serve as models* in our pleading for forgiveness and restoration after weaknesses and falls. These arguments were: *first,* that Israel was God's property, and that His past dealings had proved this (ver. 11); *secondly,* that God's own glory was involved in the deliverance of Israel in the face of the enemy (ver. 12); and, *thirdly,* that God's gracious promises were pledged for their salvation (ver. 13). And such pleas God never refuses to accept (ver. 14).

But, although informed of the state of matters in the camp of Israel, Moses could have been scarcely prepared for the sight which presented itself, when, on suddenly turning an eminence, [20] the riotous multitude, in its licentious merriment, appeared full in view. The contrast was too great, and as "Moses' wrath waxed hot, he cast the tables out of his hands, and brake them beneath the mount" (ver. 19). It is not necessary to suppose that what follows in the sacred text is related in the strict order of time. Suffice it, that, after a short but stem reproof to Aaron, Moses took his station "in the gate of the camp," summoning to him those who were "on the side of Jehovah." All the sons of

Levi obeyed, and were directed to go through the camp and "slay every man his brother, and every man his companion, and every man his neighbour" (ver. 27). On that terrible day no less than 3,000 men fell under the sword of Levi. As for the Golden Calf, its wooden framework was burnt in the fire and its gold covering ground to powder, and strewed upon the brook which descended from Sinai. [21] Of this Israel had to drink, in symbol that each one must receive and bear the fruits of his sin, just as, later on, the woman suspected of adultery was ordered to drink the water into which the writing of the curses upon her sin had been washed. [22]   There is one point here which requires more particular inquiry than it has yet received. As commonly understood, the slaughter of these 3,000 stands out as an unexplained fact. Why just *these* 3,000? Did they fall simply because they happened to stand by nearest, on the principle, as has been suggested, of decimating an offending host; and why did no one come to their aid? Such indiscriminate punishment seems scarcely in accordance with the Divine dealings. But the text, as it appears to us, furnishes hints for the right explanation. When Moses stood in the camp of Israel and made proclamation for those who were on Jehovah's side, we read that "he saw that the people were naked" (ver. 25), or unreined, *licentious* (comp. ver. 6; 1 Cor. x. 7, 8). In short, there stood before him a number of men, fresh from their orgies, in a state of licentious attire, whom even his appearance and words had not yet sobered into quietness, shame, and repentance. These, as we understand it, still thronged the open roadway of the camp, which so lately had resounded with their voices; these were met by the avenging Levites, as, sword in hand, they passed from gate to gate, like the destroying angel through Egypt on the Paschal night; and these were the 3,000 which fell on that day, while the vast multitude had retired to the quietness of their tents in tardy repentance and fear, in view of him whose presence among them betokened the nearness of that holy and jealous God, Whose terrible judgments they had so much cause to dread.

Thus ended the day of Moses' return among his people. On the morrow he gathered them to speak, not in anger but in sorrow, of their great sin. Then returning from them to the Lord, he entreated forgiveness for his brethren, with an intensity and self-denial of love (vers. 31, 32), unequalled by that of any man except St. Paul. [23] Thus far he prevailed, that the people were not to be destroyed, nor the covenant to cease; but God would not personally go in the midst of a people so incapable of bearing His holy Presence; He would send a created angel to be henceforth their leader. And still would this sin weight the scale in the day of visitation, which the further rebellion of this people would only too surely bring. The first words of the final sentence, that their carcasses were to fall in the wilderness, [24] were, so to speak, already uttered in this warning of the Lord on the morrow of the slaughter of the 3,000: "Nevertheless in the day when I visit I will visit their sin upon them." "Thus," in the language of Scripture (ver. 35), "Jehovah smote the people, because they made the calf, which Aaron made." [25]

That the Lord would not go personally with Israel because of their stiff-neckedness, was, indeed, felt to be "evil tidings." [26] The account of the people's repentance and of God's gracious forgiveness [27] forms one of the most precious portions of this history. The first manifestation of their godly sorrow was the putting away of their "ornaments," not only temporarily but permanently. Thus we read: "The children of Israel stripped themselves of their ornaments from the mount Horeb onward" (xxxiii. 6). [28] Israel was, so to speak, in permanent mourning, ever after its great national sin. Next, as the Lord would not personally be in the midst of Israel, Moses removed the tent — probably his own — outside the camp, that there he might receive the Divine communications, when "the cloudy pillar descended," "and Jehovah talked with Moses." Moses called this "the tent of meeting" (rendered in the Authorised Version "the tabernacle of the congregation:" ver. 7). It is scarcely necessary to say, that this was not "the Tabernacle" (as the Authorised Version might lead one to infer), since the latter was not yet constructed. To this "tent of meeting" all who were of the true Israel, and who regarded Jehovah not merely as their national God, but owned Him personally and felt the need of Him, were wont to go out. This must not be looked upon as either a protest or an act of separation on their part, but as evidence of true repentance and of their desire to meet with God, who no longer was in the camp of Israel. Moreover, all the people, when they saw the cloudy pillar descend to Moses, "rose up and worshipped." Altogether, this was perhaps the period of greatest heart-softening during Israel's wanderings in the wilderness.

And God graciously had respect to it. He had already assured Moses that he stood in special relationship to Him ("I know thee by name"), and that his prayer for Israel had been heard ("thou hast also found grace in My sight"). But as yet the former sentence stood, to the effect that an angel, not Jehovah Himself, was to be Israel's future guide. Under these circumstances Moses now entreated Jehovah to show him His way, that is. His present purpose in regard to Israel, adding, that if God would bring them into the Land of Promise, He would "consider that this is Thy people," and hence He their God and King. This plea also prevailed, and the Lord once more promised that His own presence would go with them, and that He Himself would give them the rest of Canaan (ver. 14; comp. Deut. iii. 20; Heb. iv. 8). And Moses gave thanks by further prayer, even more earnest than before, for the blessing now again vouchsafed (vers. 15, 16).

But one thing had become painfully evident to Moses by what had happened. However faithful in his Master's house, [29] he was but a servant; and a servant knoweth not the will of his master. The threat of destruction if Jehovah remained among Israel, and the alternative of sending with them an angel, must have cast a gloom over his future mediatorship. It was, indeed, only that of a servant, however highly favoured, not of a son. [30] Oh, that he could quite understand the Being and character of the God of Israel — see, not His likeness, but His glory! [31] Then would all become clear, and, with fuller light, joyous assurance fill his heart. That such was the real meaning of Moses' prayer, "Show me Thy glory" (ver. 18), appears from the mode in which the Lord answered it. "And He said, I will make all My goodness pass before thee, and I will proclaim the Name of Jehovah before thee." Then was Moses taught, that the deepest mystery of Divine grace lay not in God's *national,* but in His *individual* dealings, in sovereign mercy: "And I will be gracious to whom I will be gracious, and will show mercy on whom I will show mercy" (ver. 19). Yet no man could see the *face* — the full outshining of Jehovah. Neither flesh nor spirit, so long as it dwelt in the flesh, could bear such glory. While that glory passed by, God would hold Moses in a clift of the rock, perhaps in the same in which a similar vision was afterwards granted to Elijah, [32] and there He would support, or "cover" him with His hand. Only "the back parts" — the after-glory, the luminous reflection of what Jehovah really was — could Moses bear to see. But what Moses witnessed, hid in the clift of the rock, and Elijah, the representative of the prophets, saw more clearly, hiding his face in his mantle, while he worshipped, appears fully revealed to us in the Face of Jesus Christ, in Whom "the whole fulness of the Godhead dwelleth bodily."

[1] Deut. ix. 9.

[2] Ex. xxv. 1-8.

[3] Ex. xxv. 9.

[4] Ex. xxv. 10-22.

[5] Ex. xxvi.

[6] Ex. xxviii.; xxix.

[7] "Da quod jubes, et jube quod vis" — Give what Thou commandest, and command what Thou wilt; a principle, we cannot too often repeat, applicable throughout the economy of grace, where all originates with God.

[8] Ex. iv. 22, 23.

[9] Ex. xxii. 29; xxxiv. 20; Numb. iii. 12, 13, 16.

[10] Rom. xi. 16.

[11] Ex. xxx. 11-16.

[12] Ex. xxxi. iii.

[13] Ex. xxxi. 17.

[14] Ex. xxxii. 1-6.

[15] Ex. xxiv. 17.

[16] Ex. xxxii. 4.

[17] Both here and in ver. 1 the rendering should be in the *singular* ("God"), and not in the *plural* ("Gods"), as in the Authorised Version.

[18] Ex. xxxii. 21-24.

[19] Deut. ix. 14.

[20] "Often in descending this" (the so-called "Hill of the Golden Calf," close by the spot whence the Law was given), "while the precipitous sides of the ravine hid the tents from my gaze, have I heard the sound of voices from below, and thought how Joshua had said unto Moses as he came down from the mount, 'There is a noise of war in the camp.'" — Mr. Palmer in *The Desert of the Exodus,* vol. i. p. 115.

[21] Deut. ix. 21. The learned reader will find every possible suggestion in *Bocharti Hieroz.,* vol. i. pp. 349, etc."

[22] Numb. v. 24.

[23] Rom. ix. 3. "It is not easy," writes Bengel, "to estimate the love of a Moses or a Paul. Our small measure of capacity can scarcely take it in, just as an infant cannot realise the courage of a hero."

[24] Numb. xiv. 26.

[25] The text does *not* necessarily imply (as the Authorised Version would naturally suggest) that any further spe-

cial "plagues" were at that time sent upon the people.

[26] Ex. xxxiii. 4.
[27] Ex. xxxiii.
[28] So literally.
[29] Heb. iii. 5.
[30] Heb. iii. 5, 6.
[31] Ex. xxxiii. 18.
[32] I Kings xix. 9.

Chapter Thirteen

(Ex. xxxiv.-xl.)

The covenant relationship between God and Israel having been happily restored, Moses was directed to bring into the mount other two tables — this time of his own preparing — instead of those which he had broken, that God might once more write down the "ten words." [1] Again he passed forty days and forty nights on Sinai without either eating or drinking (xxxiv. 28). The communications which he received were preceded by that glorious vision of Jehovah's brightness, which had been promised to him. What he *saw* is nowhere told us; only what he *heard,* when Jehovah "proclaimed" before him what Luther aptly designates as "the sermon about the name of God." It unfolded His inmost being, as that of love unspeakable — the cumulation of terms being intended to present that love in all its aspects. And, in the words of a recent German writer: "Such as Jehovah here proclaimed, He also manifested it among Israel at all times, from Mount Sinai till He brought them into the land of Canaan; and thence till He cast them out among the heathen. Nay, even now in their banishment, He is 'keeping mercy for thousands, who turn to the Redeemer that has come out of Zion.'"

When Moses thus fully understood the character of Jehovah, he could once more plead for Israel, now converting into a plea for forgiveness even the reason which had seemed to make the presence of Jehovah among Israel dangerous — that they were a stiff-necked people (ver. 9). In the same manner had the Lord, in speaking to Noah, made the sin of man, which had erst provoked judgment, the ground for future forbearance. [2] And the Lord now graciously confirmed once more His covenant with Israel. In so doing He reminded them of its two conditions, the one negative, the other positive, but both strictly connected, and both applying to the time when Moses should be no more, and Israel had entered on possession of the Promised Land. These two conditions were always to be observed, if the covenant was to be maintained. The one was avoidance of all contact with the Canaanites and their idolatry (vers. 11-16); the other, observance of the service of Jehovah in the manner prescribed by Him (vers. 17-26).

Another confirmation of the Divine message which Moses bore from the mount, appeared on his return among Israel. All unknown to himself, the reflection of the Divine glory had been left upon him, and "the skin of his face shone [3] (shot out rays) because of His (God's) talking with him." [4] As Aaron and the children of Israel were afraid of this reflection of the Divine glory, Moses had to use a covering for his face while speaking to them, which he

88

only removed when conversing with the Lord. It is to this that the apostle refers [5] when he contrasts the Old Testament glory on the face of Moses, which "was to be done away" — at any rate at the death of Moses — and which was connected with what, after all, was "the ministration of death," with "the ministration of the Spirit" and its exceeding and enduring glory. Moreover, the vail with which Moses had to cover his face was symbolical of the vail covering the Old Testament, which is only "done away in Christ" (2 Cor. iii. 13, 14).

Everything was now ready for the construction of the Tabernacle and of all requisite for its services. We can understand how, especially in view of the work before them, the Sabbath rest should now be once more enjoined. [6] Then a proclamation was made for voluntary contributions of all that was needful, to which the people responded with such "willing offerings" (xxxv. 29), that soon not only "sufficient" but "too much" "for all the work" was gathered. [7] The amount of gold and silver actually used is expressly mentioned in Exodus xxxviii. 24-26. The sum total of the *gold* amounts in present value to at least 131,595*l.*, and that of the silver to about 75,444*l.*, or both together to 207,039*l.* And it must be borne in mind, that this sum does not indicate the whole amount offered by Israel — only that actually employed. In regard to the silver, either less of it was offered or none at all may have been required, since the 75,444*l.* in silver represent the exact amount of the "ransom money" [8] which every Israelite had to pay on their being first numbered (xxxviii. 26). Nor was it only gold, silver, and other material which the people brought. All "wise-hearted" men and women "whose heart the Lord stirred up" — that is, all who understood such work, and whose zeal was kindled by love for God's sanctuary — busied themselves, according to their ability, under the direction of Bezaleel, the grandson of Hur, and Aholiab, of the tribe of Dan. But what chiefly impresses us in the sacred narrative is the evidence of spiritual devotion, which appeared alike in the gifts and in the labour of the people. "And Moses did look upon all the work, and, behold, they had done it as Jehovah had commanded, even so had they done it: and Moses blessed them." [9]

Under such willing hands, the whole work was completed within an almost incredibly short period. On comparing Exodus xix. 1, which fixes the arrival of Israel at Mount Sinai as in the third month (of the first year), with Exodus xl. 2, which informs us that the Tabernacle was ready for setting up "on the first day of the first month" (of the second year), we find that an interval of nine months had elapsed. From this, however, must be deducted twice forty days, during which Moses was on the mount, as well as the days when Israel prepared for the covenant, and those when it was ratified and the law given, and also the interval between Moses' first and second stay on the mountain. Thus the whole of the elaborate work connected with the Tabernacle and its services must have been done *within six months*. And now that "the Tabernacle was reared up," Moses first placed within the Most Holy Place the Ark holding "the testimony," and covered it with the mercy-seat; next, he ranged in the Holy Place, to the north, the table of shewbread, setting "the bread in order upon it before the Lord;" then, to the south, "the candlestick," lighting its lamps before the Lord; and finally "the golden altar" "before the vail" of the Most Holy Place, "and he burnt sweet incense thereon." All this being done, and the curtain at the entrance to the Tabernacle hung up, [10] the altar of burnt-offering was placed "by the door of the Tabernacle," and "the laver" between it and that altar, although probably not in a straight line, but somewhat to the side of the altar of burnt-offering. And on the altar smoked the burnt and the meat-offering, and the laver was filled with water, in which Moses, and Aaron, and his sons washed their hands and their feet.

All was now quite in readiness — means, ordinances, and appointed channels of blessing, and all was in waiting. One thing only was needed; but that the one upon which the meaning and the efficacy of everything depended. But God was faithful to His promise. As in believing expectancy Israel looked up, "the cloud covered the tent of the congregation, and the glory of Jehovah filled the Tabernacle." Outside, visible to all, rested "upon the tent" that Cloud and Pillar, in which Jehovah had hitherto guided them, and would continue so to do. For, as the cloud by day and the appearance of fire by night tarried over the Tabernacle, the children of Israel "abode in their tents," "and journeyed not." But, "when it was taken up," then Israel's camp speedily disappeared, and, journeying, they followed their Divine Leader (comp. Numbers ix. 15-23). A *constant, visible,* and *guiding* Presence of Jehovah this among His professing people, resting above the outer tent that covered the Tabernacle. But within that Tabernacle itself there was yet another and unapproachable Presence. For "the glory of Jehovah filled the Tabernacle. And Moses was not able to enter into the tent of the congregation, because the cloud abode thereon, and the glory of Jehovah filled the Tabernacle." [11] Presently it withdrew within the Most Holy Place, into which none could enter but the high-priest once a year, and that on the day and for the purpose of atonement, and where it rested between the cherubim of glory, above the mercyseat, that covered the ark with the testimony. For "the way into the holiest of all was not yet made manifest." "But Christ being come an high-priest of good things to come, by a greater and more perfect tabernacle, not made with hands, that is to say, not of this building; neither by the blood of goats and calves, but by His own blood He entered in once into the holy place, having obtained eternal redemption for us." [12]

[1] Ex. xxxiv. 1-4.

[2] Gen. vi. 5, 6, comp. with Gen. viii. 21.

[3] The Hebrew word is derived from *a horn*, and some versions actually translate: "he wist not that his face was *horned*." From this the representation of Moses with horns on his forehead has had its origin.

[4] So literally.

[5] 2 Cor. iii. 7.

[6] Ex. xxxv. 2, 3.

[7] Ex. xxxvi, 5-7.

[8] Ex. xxx. 12.

[9] Ex. xxxix. 43.

[10] Ex. xl. 28.

[11] Ex. xl. 34, 35.

[12] Heb. ix. 8, 11, 12.

Chapter Fourteen

(Leviticus.)

The Book of Exodus was intended to tell how the Lord God redeemed and set apart for Himself "a peculiar people." Accordingly, it appropriately closes with the erection of the Tabernacle and the hallowing of it by the visible Presence of Jehovah in the Holy Place. It yet remained to show the other aspect of the covenant. For the provisions and the means of grace must be accepted and used by those for whom they are designed, and the "setting apart" of the people by Jehovah implied, as its converse, consecration on the part of Israel. And this forms the subject matter of the Book of Leviticus, [1] which a recent German writer has aptly described as "the code regulating the spiritual life of Israel, viewed as the people of God." To sum up its general contents — it tells us in its first Part (i.-xvi.) how Israel was to *approach* God, together with what, symbolically speaking, was inconsistent with such approaches; and in its second Part (xvii.-xxvii.) how, having been brought near to God, the people were to maintain, to enjoy, and to exhibit the state of grace of which they had become partakers. Of course, all is here symbolical, and we must regard the directions and ordinances as conveying in an outward form so many spiritual truths. Perhaps we might go so far as to say, that Part I. of Leviticus exhibits, in a symbolical form, the doctrine of *justification,* and Part II. that of *sanctification;* or, more accurately: the manner of *access to God,* and the *holiness* which is the result of that access.

It has already been pointed out, that the Book of Leviticus consists of two Parts; the one ending with chapter xvi.; the other, properly speaking, with chapter xxv.; chapter xxvi. being a general conclusion, indicating the blessings of faithful adherence to the covenant, while chapter xxvii., which treats of vowing unto the Lord, forms a most appropriate *appendix.* At the close of the book itself, [2] and of the chapter which, for want of a better name, we have termed its *appendix* (xxvii. 34), we find expressions indicating the purpose of the whole, and that the book of Leviticus forms in itself a special and independent part of the Pentateuch. We repeat it: the Book of Leviticus is intended for Israel as the people of God; it is the statute-book of Israel's spiritual life; and, on both these grounds, it is neither simply legal, in the sense of ordinary law, nor yet merely ceremonial, but *throughout symbolical and typical.* Accordingly, its deeper truths apply to all times and to all men.

Part I. (i.-xvi.), which tells Israel *how to approach God so as to have communion with Him,* appropriately opens with a description *of the various kinds of sacrifices.* [3] It next treats of the priesthood. [4] The thoroughly symbolical character of all, and hence the necessity of closest adherence to the directions given, are next illustrated by the judgment which befell those who offered incense upon "strange fire." [5] From the priesthood the sacred text passes to *the worshippers.* [6] These must be clean — *personally* (xi. 1-47), in their *family-life,* [7] and *as a congregation.* [8] Above and beyond all is the *great cleansing* of the *Day of Atonement,* [9] with which the first part of the book, concerning access to God, closes.

The *Second Part* of the Book of Leviticus, which describes, in symbolical manner, the *holiness* that becometh the people of God, treats, first, of *personal holiness,* [10] then of *holiness in the family,* [11] of *holiness in social relations,* [12] and of *holiness in the priesthood.* [13] Thence the sacred text proceeds to holy seasons. [14] As the duty of close adherence to the Divine directions in connection with the priesthood had been illustrated by the judgment upon Nadab and Abihu, [15] so now the solemn duty, incumbent on all Israel, to treat the Name of Jehovah as holy, is exhibited in the punishment of one who had blasphemed it. [16] Finally, Leviticus xxv. describes the *holiness of the land.* Thus Part II. treats more especially of *consecration.* As Part I., describing access to God, had culminated in the ordinance of the Day of Atonement, so Part II. in that of the Jubilee Year. Lastly, Leviticus xxvi. dwells on the blessing attaching to faithful observance of the covenant; while Leviticus xxvii., reaching, as it were, beyond ordinary demands and consecrations, speaks of the free-will offerings of the heart, as represented by vows.

It now only remains to describe the two illustrative instances already referred to — the one connected with the priesthood, the other with the people. Aaron and his sons had just been solemnly consecrated to their holy office, and the offering, which they had brought, consumed in view of the whole people by fire from before Jehovah, to betoken His acceptance thereof. [17] All the more did any transgression of the Lord's ordinance, especially if committed by His priests, call for signal and public punishment. But *Nadab* and *Abihu,* the two eldest sons of Aaron, attempted to offer "strange fire before Jehovah, which He commanded them not." [18] Some writers have inferred from the prohibition of wine or of any strong drink to the priests during the time of their ministry, which immediately follows upon the record of this event (x. 8-11), that these two had been under some such influence at the time of their daring attempt. The point is of small importance, comparatively speaking. It is not easy to say what the expression "strange fire" exactly implies. Clearly, the two were going to offer incense on the golden altar (ver. 1), and as clearly this service was about to be done at a time *not* prescribed by the Lord. For a comparison of vers. 12 and 16 shows that it took place between the sacrifice offered by Aaron [19] and the festive meal following that sacrifice; whereas incense was only to be burnt at the morning and evening sacrifices. Besides, it may be, that they also took "strange fire" in the sense of taking the burning coals otherwise than from the altar of burnt-offering. In the ceremonial for the Day of Atonement the latter is expressly prescribed, [20] and it is a fair inference that the same direction applied to every time of incensing. At any rate, we know that such was the invariable rule in the Temple at the time of Christ.

But Nadab and Abihu were not allowed to accomplish their purpose. The same fire, which a little ago had consumed the accepted sacrifice, [21] now struck them, "and they died before Jehovah," that is, in front of His dwelling-place — most probably in the court (comp. Leviticus i. 5), just as they were about to enter the Holy Place. Thus, on the very day of their consecration to the priesthood, did the oldest sons of Aaron perish, because they had not sanctified the Lord in their hearts, but had offered Him a worship of their own devising, instead of that holy incense consumed by fire from off the altar, which symbolised prayer, offered up on the ground of accepted sacrifice. And this twofold lesson did the Lord Himself teach in explanation of this judgment (x. 3). So far as the priesthood was concerned — "I will sanctify Myself in those who stand near to Me, [22] and" (so far as all the people were concerned) "before all the people I will glorify Myself." In other words, if those who had been consecrated to Him would not sanctify Him in heart and life. He would sanctify Himself in them by judgments (comp. also Ezekiel xxxviii. 16), and thus glorify His Name before all, as the Holy One, Who cannot with impunity be provoked to anger.

So deeply was Aaron solemnized, that, in the language of Scripture, he "held his peace." Not a word of complaint escaped his lips; nor yet was a token of mourning on his part, or on that of his sons, allowed to cast the shadow of personal feelings, or of latent regret, upon this signal vindication of Divine holiness (x. 6). Only their "brethren, the whole house of Israel" were permitted to "bewail this burning (of His anger) which Jehovah hath kindled."

The history of the judgment upon the blasphemer [23] was inserted in the portion of Leviticus where it stands, either because it happened at the time when the laws there recorded were given, or else because it forms a suitable introduction to, and illustration of, the duty of owning Jehovah, which finds its fullest outward expression in the rest of the Sabbatical and in the arrangements of the Jubilee Year, enjoined in Leviticus xxv. It also affords another instance of the dangers accruing to Israel from the presence among them of that "mixed multitude" which had followed them from Egypt. [24] There seems no reason to doubt the Jewish view, that the latter occupied a separate place in the camp; the children of Israel being ranged according to their tribes, "every man by his own standard, with the ensign of their father's house." [25] But as the blasphemer was only the son of a Danite *mother* — Shelomith, the daughter of Dibri — his father having been an Egyptian, [26] he would not have been entitled to pitch his tent among the tribe of Dan. Hebrew tradition further states, that this had been the cause of the quarrel, when the blasphemer "went out among the children of Israel; and this son of the Israelitish woman and a man of Israel strove together in the camp." Finally, it adds, that the claim to dwell among the Danites having been decided by Moses against him, the man "blasphemed the Name [27] (*of Jehovah*), and cursed." Whatever truth, if any, there be in this tradition, the crime itself was most serious. If even cursing one's parents was visited with death, what punishment could be too severe upon one who had "reviled" Jehovah, and "cursed!" But just because the case was so solemn, Moses did not rashly adjudicate in it (comp. the corresponding delay in Numbers xv. 34). "They put him in ward to determine about them (*i.e.* about blasphemers), according to the mouth (or command) of Jehovah." [28] Then by Divine direction the blasphemer was taken without the camp; those who had heard his blasphemy laid "their hands upon his head," as it were to put away the blasphemy from themselves, and lay it on the head of the guilty (comp. Deut. xxi. 6); and the whole congregation shared in the judgment by stoning him.

But the general law which decreed the punishment of death upon blasphemy [29] was to apply to native Israelites as well as to the stranger, as indeed all crimes that carried retributive punishment — specially those against the life or the person — were to be equally visited, whether the offender were a Jew or a foreigner. This is the object of the repetition of these laws in that connection. [30] For Jehovah was not a national deity, like the gods of the heathen; nor were Israel's privileges those of exceptional favour in case of offences; but Jehovah was the Holy One of Israel, and holiness became His house for ever.

[1] The Book of *Leviticus*, or about the levitical ordinances, derives its designation from the corresponding Greek term in the LXX translation, and its Latin name in the Vulgate. It corresponds to the Rabbinical designation of "Law of the Priests," and "Book of the Law of Offerings." Among the Jews it is commonly known as *Vajikra*, from the first word in the Hebrew text: "*Vajikra,*" "He called."

[2] Lev. xxvi. 46.
[3] Lev. i.-vii.
[4] Lev. viii.-x.
[5] Lev. x. 1-6.
[6] Lev. xi.-xv.
[7] Lev. xii.
[8] Lev. xiii.-xv.
[9] Lev. xvi.
[10] Lev. xvii.
[11] Lev. xviii.
[12] Lev. xix. xx.
[13] Lev. xxi. xxii.

[14] Lev. xxiii. xxiv.
[15] Lev. x. 1-6.
[16] Lev. xxiv. 10 to end.
[17] Lev. ix.
[18] Lev. x. 1.
[19] Lev. ix.
[20] Lev. xvi. 12.
[21] Lev. ix. 24.
[22] So literally.
[23] Lev. xxiv. 10-14.
[24] Ex. xii. 38.
[25] Numb. ii. 2.
[26] A very ancient Jewish tradition has it, that the father of this blasphemer was the Egyptian whom Moses slew on account of his maltreatment of an Hebrew (Ex. ii. ii, 12). Legendary details are added about the previous offences of that Egyptian, which need not be here repeated. Their evident object is, on the one hand, to render the passionate anger of Moses excusable, and, on the other, to account for the fact that an Egyptian was the father of a child of which a Hebrewess was the mother.

[27] The Rabbis and the LXX version render the expression "blasphemed" by "uttered distinctly," and Jewish traditionalism has based upon this rendering the prohibition ever to pronounce the name *Jehovah* — an ordinance so well observed that even the exact pronunciation of the word is not certainly known. Most probably it should be pronounced *Jahveh*. In our English Version, as in the LXX and Vulgate, it is rendered by "the LORD," the latter word being printed in capitals.

[28] So literally.
[29] Lev. xxiv. 16.
[30] Lev. xxiv. 17-22.

Chapter Fifteen
(Numb. i.-iv.; x. 1-11.)

The Book of Numbers [1] reads almost like a chronicle of the principal events during the thirty-eight years which elapsed between Israel's stay in the wilderness of Sinai, and their arrival on the borders of Canaan. What took place during the journey to Mount Sinai had been intended to prepare the people for the solemn events there enacted. Similarly, the thirty-eight years' wanderings which followed were designed to fit Israel for entering on possession of the Land of Promise. The outward history of the people during that period exhibited, on the one hand, the constant care and mercy of Jehovah, and on the other, His holiness and His judgments; while the laws and ordinances given them were needful for the organisation of the commonwealth of Israel in its future relations. A brief analysis of the whole book will show the connection of all.

In general, the Book of Numbers seems to consist of *three parts* — the *first,* [2] detailing *the preparations for the march* from Sinai; the second, [3] *the history of the journeyings* of Israel through the wilderness; and the *third,* [4] *the various occurrences on the east of the Jordan.* If we examine each of these parts separately, we find that Part I. *consists of four sections,* detailing — I. The numbers and the outward arrangement of each of the tribes, [5] and the appointment of the Levites to their service (iii., iv.); 2. Laws concerning the higher and spiritual order of the people, culminating in the priestly blessing (v., vi.); 3. The three last occurrences before leaving Mount Sinai (vii., viii., lx. 1-14); 4. The signals for the march in the wilderness (ix. 15-X. 10).

Part II. tells the history of the wanderings of Israel, in their three stages — 1. From Sinai to Paran, near Kadesh, detailing all that happened there (x. 10-xiv.); 2. From the announcement of the death of the generation which had come out from Egypt to the re-assembling of the people at Kadesh in the fortieth year after the Exodus (xv.-xix.); 3. The march from Kadesh to Mount Hor, with the events during its course (xx., xxi.). Lastly, Part III. *consists of five sections* detailing — 1. The attempts of Moab and Midian against Israel (xxii.-xxv.); 2. A fresh census and the ordinances connected with it (xxv.-xxvii.); 3. Certain sacred laws given in view of settling in Palestine (xxviii.-xxx.); 4. The victory over Midian, the division of the territory gained, along with a review of the past (xxxi.-xxxiii. 49); 5. Some prospective directions on taking possession of the Land of Promise (xxxiii. 50-xxxvi.). [6]

Before leaving the encampment at Mount Sinai, God directed Moses and Aaron to take a *census* of all who constituted the host of Israel — in the language of Scripture: "All that are able to go forth to war," "their armies," [7] that is, "every male from twenty years old and upwards." In this they were to be assisted by one delegate from each tribe, "every one head of the house of his fathers" (i. 4); or, as they are designated in ver. 16, "the called (representatives) of the congregation, princes of their paternal tribes, heads of thousands in Israel." [8] The latter expression indicates that the census was taken on the plan proposed by Jethro, [9] by which Israel was arranged into thousands, hundreds, fifties, and tens. This also accounts for the *even numbers* assigned to each tribe as the final result of the numbering. Manifestly, the census was made on the basis of the poll taken, nine months before, for the purpose of the "atonement money." [10] This poll had yielded a total of 603,550, [11] which is precisely the same number as that in Numbers i. 46. Probably, therefore, the census was substantially only a re-arrangement and registration of the people according to their tribes, in thousands, hundreds, fifties, and tens, made with the co-operation of the hereditary rulers of the tribes. The above number of men capable of bearing arms would, if we may apply modern statistical results, imply a total population of upwards of *two millions*. Thirty-eight years later, just before entering upon possession of the land, a second census was taken, [12] which yielded a total number of 601,730 capable of bearing arms (xxvi. 51), thus showing a decrease of 1820 during the years of wandering in the wilderness. Arranging these two census according to the tribes, and placing them side by side, we gather some interesting information: [13]

	First Census (Ex. xxx. ; Numb. i.).				Second Census (Numb. xxvi.).
REUBEN	46,500	(Prince *Elizur*, "My God the Rock.")			43,730
Simeon	59,300	(,, *Shelumiel*, "God my Salvation.")			22,200
Gad	45,650	(,, *Eliasaph*, "My God that gathers.")			40,500
JUDAH	74,600	(,, *Nahshon*, "The Diviner.")			76,500
Issachar	54,400	(,, *Nethaneel*, "God the Giver.")			64,300
Zebulon	57,400	(,, *Eliab*, "My God the Father.")			60,500
EPHRAIM	40,500	(,, *Elishama*, "My God the Hearer.")			32,500
Manasseh	32,200	(,, *Gamaliel*, "My God the Rewarder.")			52,700
Benjamin	35,400	(,, *Abidan*, "My Father is Judge.")			45,600
DAN	62,700	(,, *Ahiezer*, "My Brother is Help.")			64,400
Asher	41,500	(,, *Pagiel*, either "My fate is God," or "My prayer-God.")			53,400
Naphtali	53,400	(,, *Ahira*, "My Brother is Friend.")			45,400
	603,550				601,730

A comparison of the foregoing figures will show, that, while some of the tribes remarkably *increased,* others equally remarkably *decreased,* during the thirty-eight years' wanderings. Thus, for example, Issachar *increased* nineteen *per cent.,* Benjamin and Asher twenty-nine *per cent.,* and Manasseh about sixty-three *per cent.*; [14] while Reuben *decreased* six *per cent.,* Gad *twelve per cent.,* Naphtali fifteen *per cent.,* and Simeon almost sixty-three *per cent.* Some interpreters have connected the large decrease in the latter tribe with the judgment following upon the service of Baal Peor; the fact that Zimri, a prince of the tribe of Simeon, had been such a notable offender [15] leading to the inference that the tribe itself had been largely implicated in the sin.

It has already been noted, that the Levites were taken for the ministry of the sanctuary in place of the firstborn of Israel. [16] The number of the latter amounted to 22,273. [17] But this statement is not intended to imply that, among all the Jewish males, amounting to upwards of a million [18] of all

96

ages — from the grandfather to the infant lately born — there were only 22,273 "firstborns." The latter figure evidently indicates only the number of the firstborn since the departure from Egypt. With reference to those born previously to the Exodus we are expressly told: [19] "all the firstborn are Mine; on the day that I smote all the firstborn of Egypt I hallowed unto Me all the firstborn in Israel." Hence the fresh hallowing of the firstborn of Israel, and their subsequent numbering with a view to the substitution of the Levites for them, must have dated from *after the Paschal night.* Thus the 22,273 firstborn sons, for whom the Levites were substituted, represent those born after the departure from Egypt. If this number seems proportionally large, it should be remembered that the oppressive measures of Pharaoh would tend to diminish the number of marriages during the latter part of Israel's stay in Egypt, while the prospect of near freedom would, in a corresponding manner, immensely increase them. [20] Besides, it is a well-known fact that even now the proportion of boys to girls is very much greater among Jews than among Gentiles. [21] Viewed in this light, the account of Scripture on this subject presents no difficulties to the careful reader. [22]

As already explained, the Levites were not numbered with the other tribes, but separately, [23] and appointed ministers to Aaron the priest "for the service of the Tabernacle," in room of the firstborn of Israel (iii. 5-13). Not being regarded as part of the *host,* they were counted "from a month old and upward," the number of their males amounting to 22,000, which at the second census (after the thirty-eight years' wanderings) had increased to 23,000. [24] This has been computed to imply about 13,000 men, from twenty years and upwards — a number less than half that of the smallest of the other tribes (Benjamin, 35,400). With this computation agrees the statement [25] that the number of Levites "from thirty years old and upwards, even unto fifty years old, every one that came to do the service of the ministry," amounted in all to 8,580. [26] The same proportion between Levi and the rest of the people seems to have continued in after times, as we gather from the results of the census taken by King David, [27] when Levi had only increased from 23,000 to 38,000, while the rest of the tribes had more than doubled. The Levites were arranged into families after their ancestors, *Gershon, Kohath,* and *Merari,* the three sons of Levi. [28] The *Gershonites* (again subdivided into two families, and amounting to 7,500), under their leader Eliasaph — "My God that gathers" [29] — had charge of "the Tabernacle," or rather of "the dwelling-place;" of "the tent;" of "the covering thereof;" and of "the hanging (or curtain) for the door of the tent of meeting;" as also of "the hangings of the court" (in which the Tabernacle stood); of the curtain for its door; and of all the cordage necessary for these "hangings." We have been particular in translating this passage, because it proves that the common view, which places the curtains "of fine twined linen, and blue, and purple, and scarlet," [30] *outside* the boards that constituted the framework of the Tabernacle, is entirely erroneous. Evidently, *these hangings,* and not the boards, constituted "the Tabernacle," or rather "the dwelling" [31] — "the tent," outside the framework, consisting of the eleven curtains of goats' hair, [32] and "the covering" of the whole being twofold — one "of rams' skins dyed red," and another "of badgers' skins." [33]

Whilst the Gershonites had charge of "the dwelling," "the tent," and the hangings of the outer court, the care of the "boards of the dwelling," with all that belonged thereto, and of "the pillars of the court round about" — in short, of all the outer solid framework of the Tabernacle and of the court — devolved upon the Merarites, under their chief, Zuriel ("My Rock is God"). Finally, the most important charge — that of the contents and vessels of the sanctuary — was committed to the Kohathites, under their chief Elizaphan ("My God watcheth round about").

Viewed as a whole, the camp of Israel thus formed a threefold square — a symbolical design, further developed in the Temple of Solomon, still more fully in that of Ezekiel, and finally shown in all its completeness in "the city that lieth foursquare." [34] The innermost square — as yet elongated and therefore not perfect in its *width* (or comprehension), nor yet having the perfect form of a cube, except so far as the Most Holy Place itself was concerned (which was a cube) — was occupied by "the dwelling," covered by "the tent," and surrounded by its "court." Around this inner was another square, occupied by the ministers of the Tabernacle — in the *East,* or at the entrance to the court, by Moses, Aaron, and his sons; in the *South* by the Kohathites, who had the most important Levitical charge; in the *West* by the Gershonites; and in the *North* by the *Merarites.* Finally, there was a third and outermost square, which formed the camp of Israel. The *eastern* or most important place here was occupied by *Judah,* bearing the standard of the division. With Judah were Issachar and Zebulon (the sons of Leah), the three tribes together a host of 186,400 men. The *southern* place was held by *Reuben*, with the standard of that division, camped probably nearest to Zebulon, or at the south-eastern corner. With Reuben were Simeon and Gad (the sons of Leah and of Zilpah, Leah's maid), forming altogether a host of 151,450 men. The *western* post was occupied by *Ephraim*, with the standard of his division, being probably camped nearest to Gad, or at the south-western corner. With Ephraim were Manasseh and Benjamin (in short, the three descendants of Rachel), forming altogether a host of 108,100 men. Lastly, the *northern* side was occupied by *Dan*, with his standard, camping probably nearest to Benjamin, or at the north-western corner. With Dan were Asher and Naphtali (the sons of Bilhah and Zilpah), forming altogether a host of 157,600 men. This was also the order of march, Judah with his division leading, after which came Reuben, with his division, then the sanctuary with the Levites in the order of their camping, the rear consisting of the divisions of Ephraim and of Dan. The sacred text does not specially describe the *banners* carried by the four leading tribes. According to Jewish tradition they bore as emblems "the likeness of the four living creatures," seen by Ezekiel in his vision of the

Cherubim, [35] the *colour* of the standard being the same as that of the precious stones on the high-priest's breastplate, on which the names of the standard-bearing tribes were graven. [36] In that case *Judah* would have had on its standard a *lion* on a *blood-red ground* (the sardian stone or *sard*), *Reuben* the head of a man on a ground of *dark red* colour (the ruby or carbuncle), *Ephraim* the head of a bullock on a ground of hyacinth (the ligury, according to some, Ligurian amber), and *Dan* an eagle on a ground of bright yellow, like gold (the ancient chrysolith, perhaps our topaze). This, supposing the names to have been graven in the order in which the tribes camped. But Josephus and some of the Rabbis range the names on the breastplate in the same order as on the ephod of the high-priest, [37] that is, "according to their birth." In that case Reuben would have been on the sardian stone or sard, *Judah* on the ruby or carbuncle, Dan on a sapphire, or perhaps lapis-lazuli (blue), and *Ephraim* on an onyx, or else a beryl, [38] the colour of the banners, of course, in each case corresponding. Altogether the camp is supposed to have occupied about three square miles.

The direction either for marching or for resting was, as explained in a former chapter, given by the Cloud in which the Divine Presence was. But for actual signal to move, two silver trumpets were to be used by the sons of Aaron. A prolonged alarm indicated the commencement of the march. At the first alarm the eastern, at the second the southern part of the camp was to move forward, then came the Tabernacle and its custodians, the western, and finally the northern part of the camp, Naphtali closing the rear. On the other hand, when an assembly of the people was summoned, the signal was only *one blast* of the trumpets in short, sharp tones. In general, and for all times, the blast of these silver trumpets, whether in war, on festive, or on joyous occasions, had this spiritual meaning: "ye shall be remembered before Jehovah your God." [39] In other words, Israel was a host, and as such summoned by blast of trumpet. But Israel was a host of which Jehovah was Leader and King, and the trumpets that summoned this host were silver trumpets of the sanctuary, blown by the priests of Jehovah. Hence these their blasts brought Israel as the Lord's host in remembrance before their God and King.

[1] This designation of the Fourth Book of Moses, from the numbering of the people, is derived from its title in the LXX and in the Vulgate translation. The Jews commonly call it either *Vajedabber,* from the first word in the text, "And He (the Lord) spake;" or else *Bamidbar,* "in the wilderness."

[2] Numb. i.-x. 10.

[3] Numb. x. ii.-xxi.

[4] Numb. xxii.-xxvi.

[5] Numb. i., ii.

[6] We have substantially followed the arrangement of Keil, which agrees with that of the best modern commentators. In our remarks as to the numbering of the tribes, we have also availed ourselves of the same help.

[7] Numb. i. 3.

[8] This is the real meaning of the passage.

[9] Ex. xviii. 21, 25.

[10] Ex. xxx. 11-16.

[11] Ex. xxxviii. 26.

[12] Numb. xxvi.

[13] The names printed in capitals are those of the standard-bearers (see further on). It will be seen that of the twelve princes he of Judah bears a peculiar name. The name *Nahshon* is derived from a *serpent*. Without indulging in fanciful speculations, we may be allowed to suggest that this *may* bear prophetic reference to the Great Prophet who was to bruise the head of the *serpent*. With this also agrees the name of his father *Amminadab*, "my people is noble."

[14] The variations in population are very remarkable.

[15] Numb. xxv. 6-14.

[16] Numb. iii. 11, 12.

[17] Numb. iii. 43.

[18] The total number of the people being computed at about two millions, about one million of males would be the ordinary proportion.

[19] Numb. iii. 13; viii, 17.

[20] It is indeed unsafe to draw from *present* statistical *data* definite inferences as to the state of Israel at that time. But nothing is so remarkable as the influence of outward circumstances upon the annual number of marriages. Thus in Austria there were, in 1851, 361,249 marriages among a population of 36½ millions; while in 1854, among a population of upwards of 37 millions, only 279,202 occurred. In England the population increased between 1866 and 1869 by about a million, while in the latter year there were nearly 11,000 marriages less than in the former.

[21] The proportion of boys to girls born in England varies most curiously from year to year, and in different counties. The lowest during the last ten years has been in Huntingdonshire in the year 1868, when it descended to 94.3 boys to 100 girls. But the mean proportion during the last ten years shows from 102 to 106 boys (the latter number in Cornwall) to 100 girls. In the year 1832 the proportion in Geneva was 157 boys born to 100 girls. Among the Jews in some places the *mean* proportion has, on an average of 16 years, been as high as 145 boys to 100 girls. The reader who is curious on this and similar subjects is referred to my article, "On certain Physical Peculiarities of the Jewish Race," in the *Sunday Magazine* for 1869, pp. 315, etc.

[22] The views of the Jews on the redemption of the firstborn at the time of Christ differed from those of the Bible. See my *Temple, its Ministry and Services at the time of Christ,* p. 302.

[23] Numb. iii. 15.

[24] Numb. iii. 39; xxvi. 62.

[25] Numb. iv. 48.

[26] We cannot here enter into further numerical details. But this we can and do assert, that all supposed difficulties on this subject vanish before a careful study of the sacred text.

[27] 1 Chron. xxiii. 3.

[28] Numb. iii. 14-43.

[29] The significance of the names of "the princes," as indicative of the spiritual hopes of Israel while in Egypt, has already been pointed out in a former chapter.

[30] Ex. xxvi. 1.

[31] So it should be rendered both in Numb. iii. 25 and in Ex. xxvi. 1, 6.

[32] Ex, xxvi. 7.

[33] Ex. xxvi, 14.

[34] Rev. xx. 9; xxi. 16. We cannot here enter further into this subject. But the symbolism of the threefold square, and the symbolical meaning of the prophetic visions in Ezekiel and the Book of Revelation will readily present themselves to the thoughtful student of Scripture.

[35] Ezek. i, 10.

[36] Ex. xxviii. 15-21.

[37] Ex. xxviii. 10.

[38] It will be perceived that interpreters differ as to the exact equivalent of the precious stones mentioned in the sacred text. As to the arrangement of the stones on the high-priest's breastplate, we prefer the view that the order in the camp indicated that of the names on the breastplate.

[39] Numb. x. 1-10.

Chapter Sixteen

(Numb. vii.-ix.)

Three Other occurrences are recorded, before the camp of Israel broke up from Mount Sinai, although they may not have taken place in the exact order in which, for special reasons, they are told in the sacred text. These events were: *the offering* of certain gifts on the part of *"the princes"* of Israel; [1] the *actual setting apart of the Levites* to the service for which they had been already previously designated; [2] and a *second observance of the Passover.* [3]

The offerings of the princes of Israel commenced immediately after the consecration of the tabernacle. [4] But their record is inserted in Numbers vii., partly in order not to interrupt the consecutive series of Levitical ordinances, which naturally followed upon the narrative of the consecration of the tabernacle, [5] and partly because one of the offerings of the princes bore special reference to the wilderness-journey, which was then about to be immediately resumed. Probably these offerings may have been brought on some of the days on which part of the Levitical ordinances were also proclaimed. We know that the presentation of gifts by the princes occupied, altogether, the mornings of twelve, or rather of thirteen days. [6] On the first day [7] they brought in common "six covered waggons and twelve oxen," for the transport of the Tabernacle during the journeyings of the children of Israel. Four of these waggons with eight oxen were given to the *Merarites,* who had charge of the heavy framework and of the pillars; the other two waggons and four oxen to the *Gershonites,* who had the custody of the hangings and curtains. As for the vessels of the sanctuary, they were to be carried by the *Kohathites* on their shoulders. Then, during the following twelve days "the princes" offered successively each the same gift, that so "there might be equality," anticipating in this also the New Testament principle. [8] Each offering consisted of a "silver charger," weighing about four and a half pounds, a "silver bowl," weighing about two and a quarter pounds, both of them full of fine flour mingled with oil for a meat-offering, and a "golden spoon," about a third of a pound in weight, "full of incense." These gifts were accompanied by burnt, sin, and peace-offerings, which no doubt were sacrificed each day, as the vessels were presented in the sanctuary. And as they brought their precious offerings, with humble confession of sin over their sacrifices, with thanksgiving and with prayer, the Lord graciously signified His acceptance by speaking unto Moses "from off the mercy-seat," "from between the cherubim." [9]

The second event was *the formal setting apart of the Levites* [10] which was preceded by a significant direction to Aaron in reference to the lighting of the seven-branched candlestick in the sanctuary. To make the meaning of this symbol more clear, it was added: "the seven lamps shall give light over against the candlestick" — that is, each of the seven lamps (the number being also significant) shall be so placed as to throw its light into the darkness *over against it*. Each separately — and yet each as part of the one candlestick in the Holy Place, and burning the same sacred oil, was to shed light into the darkness over against the candlestick. For the light on the candlestick was symbolical of the mission of Israel as the people of God, and the Levites were really only the representatives of all Israel, having been substituted instead of their firstborn. [11] On this account, also, the Levites were not specially "hallowed," as the priests had been, [12] but only "cleansed" for their ministry, and after that presented to the Lord. The first part of this symbolical service consisted in sprinkling on them "water of sin" (rendered in our Authorised Version "water of purifying"), alike to confess the defilement of sin and to point to its removal. After that they were to shave off all their hair and to wash their clothes. The Levites were now "unsinned" (viii. 21), [13] so far as their persons were concerned. Then followed their dedication to the work. For this purpose the Levites were led "before the Tabernacle" (viii. 9), that is, probably into the outer court, bringing with them two young bullocks — the one for a burnt, the other for a sin-offering, and each with its meat-offering. The people, through their representatives — the princes — now laid their hands upon them, as it were to constitute them their substitutes and representatives. Then Aaron took them "before Jehovah" (ver. 10), that is, into the Holy Place, and "waved them for a wave-offering of the children of Israel" [14] — probably by leading them to the altar and back again — after which, the Levites would lay their hands upon the sacrifices which were now offered by Aaron, who so "made an atonement for them" (ver. 21). The significance of all these symbols will be sufficiently apparent. "And after that, the Levites went in to do service in the Tabernacle of the congregation" (ver. 22).

The third event recorded was a second celebration of the Passover on the anniversary of Israel's deliverance from Egypt — "in his appointed season, according to all the rites of it, and according to all the ceremonies thereof." [15] We specially mark how the Lord now again directed all — the injunction to "keep the Passover" being expressly repeated here, perhaps to obviate the possibility of such a misunderstanding as that the Passover was not to be observed from year to year. Again, when certain men, "defiled by a dead body," complained that they had thereby been excluded from the feast, Moses would not decide the matter himself, but brought their case before God. The direction given was, that, under such or similar circumstances, the Passover should be observed exactly a month later, it being at the same time added, to guard against any wilful, not necessary, neglect, that whoever omitted the ordinance without such reason should "be cut off from among His people." [16] For, as the significance of symbolical rites depended upon their entirety, so that if any part of them, however small, had been omitted, the whole would have been nullified, so, on the other hand, Israel's compliance with the prescribed rites required to be complete in every detail to secure the benefits promised to the obedience of faith. But not to receive these benefits was to leave an Israelite outside the covenant, or exposed to the Divine judgment. More than that, being caused by unbelief or disobedience, it involved the punishment due to open rebellion against God and His Word.

[1] Numb. vii.

[2] Numb. viii.

[3] Numb. ix. 1-14.

[4] Lev. viii. 10-ix. 1; comp. Numb. vii. 1.

[5] Lev. xi. to the end of the book.

[6] With the help of a Paragraph Bible it would be easy to arrange the Levitical ordinances (Lev. xi.-end) in twelve or thirteen sections for as many days.

[7] Numb. vii. 1-9.

[8] 2 Cor. viii. 14.

[9] Numb. vii. 89.

[10] Numb. viii, 5, etc.

[11] Numb. iii, 11-13.

[12] We read in Ex, xxix. 1, in reference to Aaron and his sons, "Hallow them to minister unto Me in the priest's office" — literally, "consecrate them to priest unto Me" (we use the word "priest" as a verb). In the case of the Levites there was neither consecration nor priesting, but cleansing unto ministry or service. Of course, the Aaronic priesthood pointed to and has ceased in Christ, our one great High-Priest.

[13] This is the literal rendering of the Hebrew term, which is the same as that used by David in Ps. li. 9.

[14] Rendered in our Authorised Version, "Aaron shall offer the Levites for an offering."

[15] Numb. ix. 3.

[16] Numb. ix. 13.

Chapter Seventeen

(Numb. x. 29-xi.)

At length, on the twentieth day of the second month, [1] the signal for departure from Sinai was given. The cloud which had rested upon the Tabernacle moved; the silver trumpets of the priests summoned "the camps" of Israel to their march, and as the Ark itself set forward, Moses, in joyous confidence of faith, spake those words of mingled prayer and praise which, as they marked the progress of Israel towards the Land of Promise, have ever been the signal in every forward movement of the Church [2]

> Arise, O Jehovah, let Thine enemies be scattered:
> Let them also that hate Thee flee before Thee.

The general destination of Israel was, in the first place, "the wilderness of Paran," a name known long before. [3] This tract may be described as occupying the whole northern part of the Sinaitic peninsula, between the so-called Arabah [4] on the east, and the wilderness of Shur in the west, [5] which separates Philistia from Egypt. Here Israel was, so to speak, hedged in by the descendants of Esau — on the one side by the Edomites, whose country lay east of the Arabah, and on the other by the Amalekites, while right before them were the Amorites. The whole district still bears the name Bádi-et et Tíh, "the desert of the wanderings." Its southern portion seems, as it were, driven in wedgewise into the Sinaitic peninsula proper, from which it is separated by a belt of sand. Ascending from the so-called Tor, which had been the scene of the first year of Israel's pilgrimage and of the Sinaitic legislation, the Tíh might be entered by one of several passes through the mountains which form its southern boundary. The Et Tíh itself "is a limestone plateau of irregular surface." [6] It may generally be described as "open plains of sand and gravel...broken by a few valleys," and is at present "nearly water-less, with the exception of a few springs, situated in the larger wádies," which, however, yield rather an admixture of sand and water than water. "The ground is for the most part hard and unyielding, and is covered in many places with a carpet of small flints, which are so worn and polished ... as to resemble pieces of black glass." In spring, however, there is a scanty herbage even here, while in the larger wádies there is always sufficient for camels, and even "a few patches of ground available for cultivation." Such was "that great and terrible wilderness, wherein were fiery serpents, and scorpions, [7] and drought, where there was no water," [8] through which Jehovah their God safely led Israel!

A still earlier retrospect on the part of Moses brings the events about to be described most vividly before us. Addressing Israel, he reminds them: [9] "when we departed from Horeb, we went through all that great and terrible wilderness, which ye saw by the way of the mountain of the Amorites, as Je-hovah our God commanded us; and we came to Kadesh-barnea." This "mountain of the Amorites" is the most interesting spot in the whole Et Tíh, or "wilderness of the wanderings." Arrived there, it seemed as if Israel were just about to take possession of the Promised Land. Thence the spies went forth to view the land. But here also the sentence was spoken which doomed all that unbelieving, faint-hearted generation to fall in the wilderness, and thith-er Israel had to return at the end of their forty years' wanderings to start, as it were, anew on their journey of possession. "The mountain of the Amorites" is a mountain plateau in the north-east of the Et Tíh, about seventy miles long, and from forty to fifty broad, which extends northward to near Beer-sheba. It contains many spots known to us from patriarchal history, and also celebrated afterwards. According to the description of travellers, we are here, literally, in a land of ruins, many of them dating far back, perhaps from the time of the Exodus, if not earlier. Even the old name of the Amorites is still everywhere preserved as 'Amir and 'Amori. It leaves a peculiar impression on the mind to find not only the old Scripture names of towns continued these thousands of years, but actually to hear the wells which Abraham and Isaac had dug still called by their ancient names! About half way towards Beersheba the whole character of the scenery changes. Instead of the wilderness we have now broad valleys, with many and increasing evidences of former habitation all around. Indeed, we are now in the *Negeb,* or "south coun-try" (erroneously rendered "the south" in our Authorised Version), which extends from about Kadesh to Beersheba. If "certain primeval stone remains" found throughout the Sinaitic peninsula have been regarded by the latest travellers as marking the journeyings, or rather the more prolonged settle-ments of Israel in "the wilderness," there is one class of them which deserves special attention. These are the so-called "Hazeroth," or "fenced enclosures," consisting of "a low wall of stones in which thick bundles of thorny acacia are inserted, the tangled branches and long needle-like spikes forming a perfect-ly impenetrable hedge around the encampment "of tents and cattle which they sheltered. These "Hazeroth," so frequently referred to in Scripture, abound in this district.

Such then was the goal and such the line of march before Israel, when, on that day in early summer, the Ark and the host of the Lord moved forward from the foot of Sinai. At the reiterated request of Moses, Hobab, the brother-in-law of Moses, had consented to accompany Israel, and to act as their guide in the wilderness, in the faith of afterwards sharing "what goodness Jehovah" would do unto His people. [10] This we learn from such passages as Judges i. 16; 1 Samuel xv. 6; xxvii. 10; xxx. 29. Although the pillar of cloud was the real guide of Israel in all their journeying, yet the local knowledge of Hobab would manifestly prove of the greatest use in indicating springs and places of pasturage. And so it always is. The moving of the cloud or its resting must be our sole guide; but under its direction the best means which human skill or knowledge can suggest should be earnestly sought and thankfully used.

For three days Israel now journeyed without finding "a resting-place." By that time they must have fairly entered upon the "great and terrible wilder-ness." The scorching heat of a May sun reflected by such a soil, the fatigues of such a march, with probably scarcity of water and want of pasturage for their flocks — all combined to depress those whose hearts were not strong in faith and filled with longing for the better country. Behind and around was the great wilderness, and, so far as could be seen, no "resting-place" before them! In truth, before inheriting the promises, Israel had now to pass through a trial of faith analogous to that which Abraham had undergone. Only as in his case each victory had been marked by increasing encouragements, in theirs each failure was attended by louder warnings, till at last the judgment came which deprived that unbelieving generation of their share in the enjoyment of the promise. Three days' journey under such difficulties, [11] and "the people were as they who complain of evil in the ears of Jehovah." [12] But as this really reflected upon His guidance, it displeased the Lord, and a fire, sent by Jehovah, "consumed in the ends of the camp." At the intercession of Moses "the fire was quenched." But the lesson which might have been learned, and the warning conveyed in the judgment which had begun in the uttermost parts of the camp, remained unnoticed. Even the name *Taberah* (burning), with which Moses had intended to perpetuate the memory of this event, was unheeded. Possibly, the quenching of the fire may have deadened their spiritual sensibility, as formerly the removal of the plagues had hardened the heart of Pharaoh and of his people. And so Taberah soon became *Kibroth-hattaavah,* [13] and the fire of wrath that had burned in the uttermost parts raged fiercely within the camp itself.

The sin of Israel at Kibroth-hattaavah was due to lust, and manifested itself in contempt for God's provision and in a desire after that of Egypt. The "mixed multitude" which had come up with Israel were the first to lust. From them it spread to Israel. The past misery of Egypt — even its cruel bondage — seemed for the moment quite forgotten, and only the lowest thoughts of the abundant provision which it had supplied for their carnal wants were present to their minds. This impatient question of disappointed lustfulness, "Who shall give us flesh to eat?" repeated even to weeping, can only be accounted for by such a state of feeling. But if it existed, it was natural that God's gracious provision of manna should also be despised. As if to mark their sin in this the more clearly, Scripture here repeats its description of the manna, and of its miraculous provision. [14] When Moses found "the weeping" not confined to any particular class, but general among the people (xi. 10), and that "the anger of Jehovah was kindled greatly," his heart sank within him. Yet, as has been well observed, he carried his complaint to the Lord in prayer, and therefore his was not the language of unbelief, only that of utter depression. Rightly understood, these words of his, "Have I conceived all this people? have I begotten them?" implied that not *he* but *God* was their father and their provider, [15] and that therefore he must cast their care upon the Lord. But even so the trial of Moses had in this instance become a temptation, although God gave him "with the temptation a way of escape."

Two things would the Lord do in answer to the appeal of Moses. First, He would, in His tender mercy, support and encourage His servant, and then manifest His power and holiness. With this twofold purpose in view, Moses was directed to place seventy of the elders of Israel — probably in a semicircle — around the entrance to the Tabernacle. These "elders" were henceforth to help Moses in bearing the burden of the people. He had wished help, and he was now to receive it, although he would soon experience that the help of man was vain, and God alone the true helper. And then, to show in sight of all men that He had appointed such help, *yet only as a help to Moses,* God "came down in a cloud," spake unto Moses, and then put of his spirit upon these "elders." In manifestation of this new gift "they prophesied," by which, however, we are to understand not the prediction of future events, but probably that "speaking in the spirit" which in the New Testament also is designated as "prophesying." [16] Further, lest in the mind of the people this should be connected with any miraculous power inherent in Moses, the same spirit descended, and with the same effect, upon two (Eldad and Medad) who had been "written," that is, designated for the office, but who for some reason had been prevented from appearing at the door of the Tabernacle. The lesson, it was evident, was required, for even Joshua had misunderstood the matter. When he found that Eldad and Medad prophesied "in the camp," he deemed the authority of his master compromised, and wished to "forbid them," since these men had not received the gift through Moses. We are here reminded of the similar conduct of John, who would have forbidden one "casting out devils" in the name of Christ, because he followed not with the other disciples, and of the Lord's rebuke of such mistaken zeal [17] — a mistake too often repeated, and a rebuke too much forgotten in the Christian Church at all times. Far different were the feelings of Moses. As a faithful servant, he emphatically disclaimed all honour for himself, and only expressed the fervent wish that the same spiritual gifts might be shared by all the Lord's people.

One thing was still required. God would manifest His power in providing for the wants of the people, and His holiness in taking vengeance on their lust. The lesson was specially needed, for even Moses had, when first told, questioned the full promise of providing for the whole people flesh sufficient to last for a month. [18] And now the Lord again showed how easily He can bring about supernatural results by what we call natural means. As explained in a former chapter, in spring the quails migrate in immense numbers from the interior of Africa northwards. An east wind, blowing from the Arabian Gulf, now drove them, in vast quantities, just over the camp of Israel Here they fell down exhausted by the flight, and lay, to the distance of a day's journey "on this side and on that," in some places two cubits high. It is the same lesson which we have so often learned in this history. The "wind" which brought the quails "went forth from the Lord,"' and the number brought was far beyond what is ordinarily witnessed, although such a flight and drooping of birds are by no means uncommon. And so God can, by means unthought of, send sudden deliverance — unexpectedly, even to one like Moses. But as for Israel, they had now their wishes more than gratified. The supply of flesh thus provided sufficed not only for the present, but was such that the greater part of it was preserved for after use (xi. 32). Thus had God shown the folly of those who murmured against His provision or questioned His ability. It still remained to punish the presumption and sin of their conduct. "While the flesh was yet between their teeth, ere it was chewed, the wrath of Jehovah was kindled against the people, and Jehovah smote the people with a very great plague. And he called the name of that place Kibroth-hattaavah (the graves of lust): because there they buried the people that lusted." But how deeply the impression of this judgment sunk into the hearts of the godly in Israel appears from such passages as Psalm lxxviii. 26-31, while its permanent lesson to all times is summed up in these words: "He gave them their request; but sent leanness into their soul." [19]

[1] That is, the month after the Passover; probably about the middle of May.
[2] Ps. lxviii, 1. "In order to arm the Church with confidence, and to strengthen it with alacrity against the violent attacks of enemies." — Calvin.
[3] Gen. xiv. 6; xxi. 21.

[4] The deep valley which runs from the Dead Sea to the Gulf of Akabah.
[5] Gen. xvi. 7; Ex. xv. 22.
[6] When not otherwise stated, the quotations within inverted commas are from Palmer's *Desert of the Exodus*.
[7] "In the course of the day we caught and bottled a large specimen of the cerastes, or horned snake, a very poisonous species, which abounds in the desert." — *Desert of the Exodus*, p. 310.
[8] Deut. viii. 15.
[9] Deut. i. 19.
[10] Numb. x. 32.
[11] The distance of "three days' journey" (Numb. x. 33) prevents our ac-cepting Professor Palmer's theory, who identifies Taberah with the present Erweis el Ebeirig, — *Desert of the Exodus*, pp. 257, 312.
[12] Numb. xi. I.
[13] The locality of the two is evidently the same, as appears even from the omission of Taberah from the list of encampments in Numb. xxxiii. 16.
[14] Numb. xi. 7-9.
[15] Ex. iv. 22; Isa. lxiii. 16.
[16] 1 Cor. xii.; xiv.
[17] Mark ix. 38; Luke ix. 49.
[18] Numb. xi. 18-23.
[19] Ps. cvi. 15.

Chapter Eighteen

(Numb. xii,-xiv.)

Hitherto the spirit of rebellion on the part of the people had been directed against Jehovah Himself. If Moses had lately complained of continual trials in connection with those to whom he stood in no way closely related, [1] he was now to experience the full bitterness of this: "A man's foes shall be they of his own household." [2] From Kibroth-hattaavah Israel had journeyed to Hazeroth, a station the more difficult to identify from the commonness of such "fenced enclosures" in that neighbourhood. [3] Here Miriam and — apparently at her instigation [4] — Aaron also "spake against Moses," as it is added, "because of the Ethiopian woman whom he had married," referring most likely to a second marriage which Moses had contracted after the death of Zipporah. For the first time we here encounter that pride of Israel after the flesh and contempt for all other nations, which has appeared throughout their after history, and in proportion as they have misunderstood the spiritual meaning of their calling. Thus, as Calvin remarks, Miriam and Aaron now actually boasted in that prophetic gift, which should have only wrought in them a sense of deep humility. [5] But Moses was *not* like any ordinary prophet, although in his extreme meekness he would not vindicate his own position (xii. 3). He "was faithful," or approved, "to Him that appointed him," [6] not merely in any one special matter, but "in all the house" of Jehovah, that is, in *all* pertaining to the kingdom of God. And the Lord now vindicated His servant both by public declaration, and by punishing Miriam with leprosy. At the entreaty of Aaron, who owned his sister's and his own guilt, and at the intercession of Moses, this punishment was indeed removed. But the isolation of Miriam from the camp of Israel would teach all, how one who had boasted in privileges greater than those of others might be deprived even of the ordinary fellowship of Israel's camp.

The seven days of Miriam's separation were past, and Israel again resumed the march towards the Land of Promise. They had almost reached its boundary, when the event happened which not only formed the turning-point in the history of that generation, but which, more than any other, was typical of the future of Israel. For as that generation in their unbelief refused to enter the Land of Promise when its possession lay open before them, and as they rebelled against God and cast off the authority of Moses, so did their children reject the fulfilment of the promises in Christ Jesus, disown Him whom God had exalted a Prince and a Saviour, and cry out: "Away with Him! away with Him!" And as the carcases of those who had rebelled fell in the wilderness, so has similar spiritual judgment followed upon the terrible cry: "His blood be upon us and upon our children!" But, blessed be God, as mercy was ultimately in store for the descendants of that rebellious generation, so also, in God's own time, will Israel turn again unto the Lord and enjoy the promises made unto the fathers.

The scene of this ever-memorable event was "the wilderness of Paran," or, to define the locality more exactly, *Kadesh-barnea*. [7] The spot has first been identified by Dr. Rowlands and Canon Williams, [8] and since so fully described by Professor Palmer, that we can follow the progress of events, step by step. Kadesh is the modern 'Ain Gadis, or spring of Kadesh, and lies in that north-eastern plateau of the wilderness of Paran, which formed the stronghold of the Amorites. [9] A little north of it begins the Negeb or "south country" of Palestine, [10] which, as already explained, reaches to about Beersheba, and where the Promised Land really begins. The district is suited for pasturage, and contains abundant traces of former habitation, and, in the north, also evidence of the former cultivation of vines. Here, and not, as is usually supposed, in the neighbourhood of Hebron, we must look for that valley of *Eshcol,* [11] whence the spies afterwards on their return brought the clusters of grapes, as specimens of the productiveness of the country. Kadesh itself is the plain at the foot of the cliff whence the 'Ain Gadis springs. To the east is a ridge of mountains, to the west stretches a wide plain, where the Canaanites had gathered to await the advance of Israel. Hence, if the spies were to "get up this Negeb" ("south country"), they had "to go up by the mountain," [12] in order to avoid the host of Canaan. In so doing they made a detour, passing south of 'Ain Gadis, through what is called in Scripture the wilderness of Zin (xiii. 21), from which they ascended into the mountains. Thus much seems necessary to understand the localisation of the narrative.

But to return. From Deut. i. 22, we gather that the proposal of sending spies "to search out the land" had originally come from the people. By permission of the Lord, Moses had agreed to it, [13] adding, however, a warning to "be of good courage" (Numb. xiii. 20), lest this should be associated with fear of the people of the land. Twelve persons, seemingly the most suitable for the work, — spiritually and otherwise — were chosen from "the rulers" of the tribes. [14] Of these we only know *Caleb* and *Joshua,* the "minister of

Moses," whose name Moses had formerly changed from *Hoshea*, which means "*help*," to Joshua, or "Jehovah is help." Detailed and accurate directions having been given them, the spies left the camp of Israel "at the time of the first-ripe grapes," that is, about the end of July. Thus far they were successful. Eluding the Canaanites, they entered Palestine, and searched the land to its northernmost boundary, "unto Rehob, as men come to Hamath," that is, as far as the plain of Coele-Syria. On their way back, coming from the north, they would of course not be suspected. Accordingly they now descended by Hebron, and explored the route which led into the Negeb by the western edge of the mountains. "In one of these extensive valleys — perhaps in Wády Hanein, where miles of grape-mounds even now meet the eye — they cut the gigantic cluster of grapes, and gathered the pomegranates and figs, to show how goodly was the land which the Lord had promised for their inheritance." [15] After forty days' absence the spies returned to camp. The report and the evidence of the fruitfulness of the land which they brought, fully confirmed the original promise of God to Israel. [16] But they added: [17] "Only that the people is strong which occupieth the land, and the cities fortified, very great, and also descendants of the Anak have we seen there," [18] whom, in their fear, they seem to have identified (ver. 33) with the *Nephilim* of the antediluvian world. [19]

This account produced immediate terror, which Caleb sought in vain to allay. His opposition only elicited stronger language on the part of the other "spies," culminating in their assertion, that, even if Israel were to possess the land, it was one "that eateth up its inhabitants," that is, a country surrounded and peopled by fierce races in a state of constant warfare for its possession. Thus the most trustworthy and the bravest from among their tribes, with only the exception of Caleb and of Joshua (whose testimony might be set aside on the ground of his intimate relationship to Moses), now declared their inability either to conquer or to hold the land, for the sake of which they had left the comforts of Egypt and endured the hardships and dangers of "the great and terrible wilderness!" A night of complete demoralisation followed — the result being open revolt against Moses and Aaron, direct rebellion against Jehovah, and a proposal to elect a fresh leader and return to Egypt! In vain Moses and Aaron "fell on their faces" before God in sight of all the congregation; in vain Joshua and Caleb "rent their clothes" in token of mourning, and besought the people to remember that the Presence of Jehovah with them implied certain success. The excited people only "spake" of stoning them, when of a sudden "the glory of Jehovah visibly appeared in the tent of meeting to all the children of Israel." [20] Almost had the Lord destroyed the whole people on the spot, when Moses again interposed - a type of the great Leader and Mediator of His people. With pleadings more urgent than ever before, he wrestled with God — his language in its intensity consisting of short, abrupt sentences, piled, as it were, petition on petition, but all founded on the glory of God, on His past dealings, and especially on the greatness of His mercy, repeating in reference to this the very words in which the Lord had formerly condescended to reveal His inmost Being, when proclaiming His "Name" before Moses. [21] Such plea could not remain unheeded; it was typical of the great plea and the great Pleader. But as, when long afterwards Israel called down upon themselves and their children the blood of Jesus, long and sore judgments wereto befall the stiff-necked and rebellious, even although ultimately all Israel should be saved, so was it at Kadesh. According to the number of days that the spies had searched the land, were to be the years of their wanderings in the wilderness, and of all that generation which had come out from Egypt, at the age of twenty and upwards, not one was to enter the Land of Promise, [22] but their carcases were to fall in that wilderness, with the exception of Caleb and Joshua. [23] But as for the other ten searchers of the land, quick destruction overtook them, and they "died by the plague before Jehovah."

This commencement of Divine judgment, coupled as it was with abundant evidence of its reality — especially in the immediate destruction of the ten spies, while Caleb and Joshua were preserved alive — produced an effect so strange and unlooked for, that we could scarcely understand it, but for kindred experience in all ages of the Church. It was now quite plain to Israel what they might, and certainly would have obtained, had they only gone forward. Yesterday that Land of Promise — in all its beauty and with all its riches — so close at hand as to be almost within sight of those mountain ranges, was literally theirs. To-day it was lost to them. Not one of their number was even to see it. More than that, their carcases were to fall in that wilderness! All this simply because they would not go forward yesterday! Let them do so to-day. If they had then done wrong, let them do the opposite to-day, and they would do right. Moreover, it was to Israel that God had pledged His word, and as Israel He would have brought them into the land. They were Israel still: let them now go forward and claim Israel's portion. But it was not so; and never is so in kindred circumstances. The wrong of our rebellion and unbelief is not turned into right by attempting the exact opposite. It is still the same spirit, which prompted the one, that influences the other. The obedience which is not of simple faith is of self-confidence, and only another kind of unbelief and self-righteousness. It is not the doing of this or that, nor the circumstance of outwardly belonging to Israel, which secures victory over the enemy, safety, or possession of the land. It is that "Jehovah is among us." [24] And the victory is ever that of faith. Not a dead promise to the descendants of Jacob after the flesh, but the presence of the living God among His believing Israel secured to them the benefits of the covenant. And Israel's determination to go up on the morrow, and so to retrieve the past, argued as great spiritual ignorance and unfitness, and involved as much rebellion and sin, as their former faint-heartedness and rebellion at the report of the spies.

In vain Moses urged these considerations on the people. The people "presumed [25] to go up to the head of the mountain," although Moses and the

Ark of the Covenant of Jehovah remained behind in the camp. From Kadesh it is only about twenty miles to *Hormah,* to which place their enemies afterwards "smote and discomfited them." As we know from the descriptions of travellers, increasing fertility, cultivation, and civilisation must have met the host as it advanced into the Negeb. The Israelites were in fact nearing what they must have felt home-ground — sacred to them by association with Abraham and Isaac. For a little to the north of Hormah are the wells of Rehoboth, Sitnah, and Beersheba, which Abraham and Isaac had dug, the memory of which is to this day preserved in the modern names of Ruheibeh, Shutneh, and Bir Seba. Abraham himself had "journeyed toward the Negeb, and dwelled between Kadesh and Shur," [26] and Isaac had followed closely in his footsteps. [27] And of the next occupants of the land, the Amorites, we find almost constantly recurring mementoes, and nowhere more distinctly than in the immediate neighbourhood of Hormah. From Judges i. 17, we know that that city, or probably rather the fort commanding it, had originally borne the name of Zephath, which simply means "watch-tower." The name Hormah, or "banning," was probably given it on a later occasion, when, after the attack of the king of Arad, Israel had "vowed the vow" utterly to destroy the cities of the Canaanites (Numb. xxi. 1-3). But, as Dr. Rowlands and Canon Williams have shown, the name Zephath has been preserved in the ruins of Sebaita, while Professor Palmer has discovered, close by, the ancient "watch-tower," which was a strong fort on the top of a hill commanding Sebaita. It is intensely interesting, amid the ruins of later fortifications, to come upon these primeval remains, which mark not only the ancient site of Zephath, but may represent the very fort behind which the Amorites and Canaanites defended themselves against Israel, and whence they issued to this war. As if to make it impossible to mistake this "mountain of the Amorites," the valley north of Sebaita bears to this day the name Dheigat el 'Amerin, or Ravine of the Amorites, and the chain of mountains to the south-west of the fort that of Rás Amir, "head" or top "of the Amorites." [28]

Israel had presumed to go up into this mountain-top without the presence of Jehovah, without the Ark of the Covenant, and without Moses. Yesterday they had been taught the lesson that their seeming weakness would be real strength, if Jehovah were among them. To-day they had in bitter experience to find out this other and equally painful truth — that their seeming strength was real weakness. Smitten and discomfited by their enemies, they fled "even unto Hormah."

[1] Numb. xi. 12.

[2] Matt. x. 36.

[3] For the reason mentioned in a previous chapter we are unable to accept Professor Palmer's identification of Hazeroth with 'Ain Hadherah, however interesting the notices. See *Desert of* *the Exodus,* vol. i., pp. 256, 259, 261, and vol. ii., pp. 289, 313, etc.

[4] We gather this from the name of Miriam being first mentioned, and from the fact that Numb. xii. 1 reads in the original: "And she spake, Miriam and Aaron, against Moses."

[5] Numb. xii, 2.

[6] Heb. iii. 2, 5.

[7] Numb. xiii. 26; Deut. i. 19.

[8] The merit of the discovery unquestionably belongs to Dr. Rowlands and Canon Williams. See Williams, *Holy City,* vol. i., p. 464.

[9] Kadesh was formerly called *En Mishpat,* "Well of Judgment," Gen, xiv. 7, The recurrence of the Eti in the earlier name identifies it more closely with the *'Ain* Gadis of Canon Williams, Mr. Wilton, and Professor Palmer.

[10] The rendering "south," in our Authorised Version, is apt to confuse the general reader.

[11] *Eshcol* means in Hebrew a bunch of grapes.

[12] Numb. xiii. 17, 22.

[13] Numb. xiii. 1.

[14] Not from the "princes," as appears by a comparison of names. Comp. Numb. xiii. 4-15 with i. 5, etc.; vii. 12, etc.

[15] Palmer's *Desert of the Exodus,* vol. ii., p. 512.

[16] Ex. iii. 8.

[17] Numb. xiii. 28.

[18] So literally. "The Anak" were probably a race or tribe, perhaps remnants of the original inhabitants of Palestine before the Canaanites took possession of it. The meaning of *Anak* is probably "long-necked."

[19] Gen. vi. 4. Rendered in the Authorised Version "giants," in Numb. xiii. 33.

[20] Numb. xiv. 10.

[21] Ex. xxxiii. 17, 19.

[22] It may be instructive to know that Numb. xiv. 21 should be rendered: "but as truly as I live, and all the earth shall be filled with the glory of Jehovah."

[23] As the tribe of Levi was not numbered with the rest (Numb. i.), they did not apparently fall within the designation of those who were to die in the wilderness (Numb. xiv. 29). Comp. Josh. xiv. i, etc. The Rabbis enumerate literally ten temptations on the part of Israel (Numb. xiv. 22); it need scarcely be said, very fancifully.

[24] Numb. xiv. 42.

[25] "Raised themselves up to go." This rendering seems the best. Others have translated, "they despised, so as," etc., or, "they persistently contended."

[26] Gen. xx. 1.

[27] Gen. xxvi. 17 to end.

[28] *Desert of the Exodus,* vol. ii. p. 380.

Chapter Nineteen

(Numb. xv.; xxxiii. 19-37; Deut. i. 46-11. 15; Numb. xvi., xvii.)

More than thirty-seven years of "wanderings" were now to be passed in "the wilderness of Paran," till a new generation had risen to enter on possession of the Land of Promise. Of that long period scarcely more than one single record is left us in Scripture. As a German writer observes: The host of Israel, being doomed to judgment, ceased to be the subject of sacred history, while the rising generation, in whom the life and hope of Israel now centred, had, as yet, no history of its own. And so we mark all this period rather by the death of the old than by the life of the new, and the wanderings of Israel by the graves which they left behind, as their carcasses fell in the wilderness.

Still, we may profitably gather together the various notices scattered in Scripture. First, then, we learn that Israel "abode in Kadesh many days," [1] and that thence their direction was "towards the Red Sea." [2] Their farthest halting-place from Kadesh seems to have been *Ezion-gaber,* which, as we know, lay on the so-called Elanitic Gulf of the Red Sea. Thence they returned, at the end of the forty years' wanderings, once more to "the wilderness of Zin, which is Kadesh." [3] The "stations" on their wanderings from Kadesh to Ezion-gaber are marked in Numbers xxxiii. 18-35. There are just seventeen of them, after leaving *Rithmah* — a name derived from *retem,* a broom-bush, and which may therefore signify the valley of the broom-bushes. If we rightly understand it, this was the original place of the encampment of Israel near Kadesh. In point of fact, there is a plain close to 'Ain Gadis or Kadesh which to this day bears the name of Abu Retemet. As for Kadesh itself— or the Holy Place, the place of "sanctifying" — which originally bore the name En Mish-pat, "well of judgment," [4] we imagine that it derived its peculiar name from the events that there took place, the additional designation of Barnea — Kadesh Barnea — either marking a former name of the place, or more probably meaning "the land of moving to and fro." [5] We presume that the encampment in "the broom-valley" was in all probability determined by the existence and promise of vegetation there, which, no doubt, was due to the presence of watercourses. Indeed, an examination of the names of the seventeen stations occupied by Israel during their wanderings shows, that all the encampments were similarly selected in the neighbourhood of water and vegetation. Thus we have *Rimmon-parez,* "the pomegranate breach" — perhaps the place where Korah's rebellion brought such terrible punishment; *Libnah,* "whiteness," probably from the white poplar trees growing there; *Rissah,* "dew;" *Mount Shapher,* "the mount of beauty," or "of goodliness;" *Mithcah,* "sweetness," in reference to the water; *Hashmonah,* "fatness," "fruit-fulness," where to this day there is a pool full of sweet living water, with abundant vegetation around; *Bene-jaakan,* or, as in Deut. x. 6, [6] *Beeroth Bene-Jaakan,* "the wells of the children of Jaakan," probably the wells which the Jaakanites had dug on their expulsion by the Edomites from their original homes; [7] *Jotbathah,* "goodness;" and *Ebronah,* probably "fords." The other names are either derived from peculiarities of scenery, or else from special events, as *Kehelathah,* "assembling;" *Makkeloth,* "assemblies;" *Haradah,* "place of terror," etc. [8]

The first impression which we derive, alike from the fewness of these stations, and from their situation, is, that the encampments were successively occupied for lengthened periods. More than that, we infer from the peculiar wording of some expressions in the original, that, during these thirty-eight years, the people were scattered up and down, the Tabernacle with the Levites forming, as it were, a kind of central camp and rallying-place. It is also quite certain that, at that period, the district in which the wanderings of Israel lay was capable of supporting such a nomadic population with their flocks and herds. Indeed, the presence of water, if turned to account, would always transform any part of that wilderness into a fruitful garden. In this respect the knowledge of irrigation, which the Israelites had acquired in Egypt, must have been of special use. Lastly, the people were not quite isolated. Not only were they near what we might call the direct highway between the East and Egypt, but they were in contact with other tribes, such as the Bene-jaakan. Deut. ii. 26-29 seems to imply that at times it was possible to purchase provisions and water, while Deut. ii. 7 shows that Israel had not only "lacked nothing" during "these forty years," but that they had greatly increased in substance and wealth. Such passages as Deut. viii. 14, etc.; xxix. 5; and Neh. ix. 21 prove in what remarkable manner God had cared for all the wants of His people during that period; and there can be no doubt that in the prophetic imagery of the future, especially by Isaiah, there is frequent retrospect to God's gracious dealings with Israel in the wilderness. [9]

Brief as is the record of these thirty-eight years, it contains a notice of two events — both in rebellion against the Lord. The first gives an account of a man who had openly violated the Divine law by gathering "sticks upon the Sabbath day." [10] Although the punishment of death had been awarded to such a "presumptuous sin," [11] the offender was, in the first place, "put in ward," partly to own the Lord by specially asking His direction, since only the punishment itself but not its mode had been previously indicated, and partly perhaps to impress all Israel with the solemnity of the matter. Due observance of the Lord's day was, indeed, from every point of view, a question of deepest importance to Israel, and the offender was, by Divine direction, "brought without the camp, and stoned with stones, and he died." We are not told at what particular period of the wanderings of Israel this event had occurred. It is apparently inserted as an instance and illustration, immediately after the warning against "presumptuous sins" (literally, "sins with a hand uplifted," viz., against Jehovah). These sins in open contempt of God's word involved the punishment of being "cut off" from the people of the Lord.

Nor have we any precise date by which to fix the other and far more serious instance of rebellion on the part of Korah and of his associates, [12] in which afterwards the people, as a whole, were implicated. [13] There is, however, reason to suppose that it occurred at an early period of "the wanderings" — perhaps, as already suggested, at Rimmon-parez. The leaders of this rebellion were Korah, a Levite — a descendant of Izhar, the brother of Amram, [14] and therefore a near relative of Aaron — and three Reubenites, Dathan, Abiram, and On. But as the latter is not further mentioned, we may suppose that he early withdrew from the conspiracy. These men gained over to their side no fewer than two hundred and fifty princes from among the other tribes, [15] all of them members of the national representative council, [16] and "men of renown," or, as we should express it, well-known leading men. Thus the movement assumed very large proportions, and evidenced wide-spread disaffection and dissatisfaction. The motives of this conspiracy seem plain enough. They were simply jealousy and disappointed ambition, though the rebels assumed the language of a higher spirituality. As descended from a brother of Aaron, Korah disliked, and perhaps coveted, what seemed to him the supremacy of Aaron, for which he could see no valid reason. He had also a special grievance of his own. True, he was one of that family of the Kohathites to whom the chief Levitical charge in the sanctuary had been committed; but then the Kohathites numbered four families, [17] and the leadership of the whole was entrusted not to any of the older branches, but to the youngest, the Uzzielites (Numb. iii. 30). Was there not manifest wrong and injustice in this, probably affecting Korah personally? It speaks well for the Levites as a whole, that, notwithstanding all this, Korah was unable to inveigle any of them in his conspiracy. But close to the tents of the Kohathites and of Korah was the encampment of the tribe of Reuben, who held command of the division on the south side of the camp. Possibly — and indeed the narrative of their punishment seems to imply this — the tent of Korah and those of the Reubenite princes, Dathan, Abiram, and On, were contiguous. And Reuben also *had* a grievance; for was not Reuben Jacob's firstborn, who should therefore have held the leadership among the tribes? It was not difficult to kindle the flame of jealousy in an Eastern breast. What claim or right had Moses, or rather the tribe of Levi whom he represented, to supremacy in Israel? Assuredly this was a grievous wrong and an intolerable usurpation, primarily as it affected Reuben, and secondarily all the other tribes. This explains the ready participation of so many of the princes in the conspiracy, the expostulation of Moses with Korah (xvi. 8-11), and his indignant appeal to God against the implied charges of the Reubenites (ver. 15). Indeed, the conspirators expressly stated these views as follows (ver. 3): "Sufficient for you!" — that is. You, Moses and Aaron, have long enough held the priesthood and the government; "for the whole congregation, all are holy, and in the midst of them Jehovah. And why exalt ye yourselves over the convocation [18] of Jehovah?" It will be observed that the pretence which they put forward to cover their selfish, ambitious motives was that of a higher spirituality, which recognised none other than the spiritual priesthood of all Israel. But, as we shall presently show, their claim to it was not founded on the typical mediatorship of the high-priest, but on their standing as Israel after the flesh.

The whole of this history is so sad, the judgment which followed it so terrible — finding no other parallel than that which in the New Testament Church overtook Ananias and Sapphira — and the rebellion itself is so frequently referred to in Scripture, that it requires more special consideration. The rebellion of Korah, as it is generally called, from its prime mover, was, of course, an act of direct opposition to the appointment of God. But this was not all. The principle expressed in their gainsaying (ver. 3) ran directly counter to the whole design of the old covenant, and would, if carried out, have entirely subverted its typical character. It was, indeed, quite true that all Israel were holy and priests, yet not in virtue of their birth or national standing, but through the typical priesthood of Aaron, who "brought them nigh" and was their intermediary with God. Again, this priesthood of Aaron, as indeed all similar selections— such as those of the place where, and the seasons when God would be worshipped, of the composition of the incense, or of the sacrifices — although there may have been secondary and subordinate reasons for them, depended in the first place and mainly upon God's appointment. "Him whom the Lord hath chosen will He cause to come near unto Him" (xvi. 5); "whom the Lord doth choose, he shall be holy" (ver. 7). Every other service, fire, or place than that which *God* had chosen, would, however well and earnestly intended, be "strange" service, "strange" fire, and a "strange" place. This was essential for the *typical* bearing of all these arrangements. It was God's appointment, and not the natural fitness of a person or thing which here came into consideration. If otherwise, they would have been natural *sequences,* not *types* — constituting a rational rather than a Divine service. It was of the nature of a type that God should appoint the earthly emblem with which He would connect the spiritual reality. The moment Israel deviated in any detail, however small, they not only rebelled against God's appointment, but destroyed the meaning of the whole by substituting the human and natural for the Divine. The types were, so to speak, mirrors of God's own fitting, which exhibited, as already present, future spiritual realities with all their blessings. In Christ all such types have ceased, because the reality to which they pointed has come.

This digression seemed necessary, alike for the proper understanding of the history of Korah and for that of the typical arrangements of the Old Testament. But to return. On the morning following the outbreak of the rebellion, Korah and his two hundred and fifty associates presented themselves, as Moses had proposed, at the door of the Tabernacle. Here "they took every man his censer, and put fire in them, and laid incense thereon." Indeed, Korah had gained such influence, that he was now able to gather there "all the congregation" as against Moses and Aaron. Almost had the wrath of God, Whose glory visibly appeared before all, consumed "this congregation" in a moment, when the intercession of Moses and Aaron once more prevailed. In these words: "O God, the God of the spirits of all flesh, shall one man sin, and wilt Thou be wroth with all the congregation?" (as Calvin remarks) Moses made his appeal "to the general grace of creation," praying that, "as God was the Creator and Maker of the world, He would not destroy man whom He had created, but rather have pity on the work of His hands." And so there is a plea for mercy, and an unspeakable privilege even in the fact of being the creatures of such a God!

Leaving the rebels with their censers at the door of the Tabernacle — perhaps panic-struck — Moses next repaired to the tents of Dathan and Abiram, accompanied by the elders, and followed by the congregation. [19] On the previous day the two Reubenites had refused to meet Moses, and sent him a taunting reply, suggesting that he only intended to blind the people. [20] And now when Dathan and Abiram, with their wives and children, came out and stood at the door of their tents, as it were, to challenge what Moses could do, the people were first solemnly warned away from them. Then a judgment, new and unheard of, was announced, and immediately executed. The earth opened her mouth and swallowed up these rebels and their families, with all that appertained to them, that is, with such as had taken part in their crime. As for Korah, the same fate seems to have overtaken him. But it is an emphatic testimony alike to the truth of God's declaration, that He punisheth not men for the sins of their fathers, [21] and to the piety of the Levites, that the sons of Korah did not share in the rebellion of their father, and consequently died not with him. [22] More than this, not only were Samuel and afterwards Heman descendants of Korah, [23] but among them were some of those "sweet singers of Israel," whose hymns. Divinely inspired, were intended for the Church at all times. And all the Psalms "of the sons of Korah" [24] have this common characteristic, which sounds like an echo of the lesson learned from the solemn judgment upon their house, that their burden is praise of the King Who is enthroned at Jerusalem, and longing after the services of God's sanctuary. [25] But as for "the two hundred and fifty men that offered incense," "there came out a fire from the Lord and consumed" them, as, on a former occasion, it had destroyed Nadab and Abihu. [26] Their censers, which had been "hallowed," by being presented before the Lord, [27] were converted into plates for covering the altar of burnt offering, that so they might be a continual "memorial unto the children of Israel" of the event and its teaching.

This signal judgment of God upon the rebels had indeed struck the people who witnessed it with sudden awe, but it led not to that repentance [28] which results from a change of heart. The impression passed away, and "on the morrow" nothing remained but the thought that so many princes of tribes, who had sought to vindicate tribal independence, had been cut off" for the sake of Moses! It was in their cause, the people would argue, that these men had died; and the mourning in the tents of the princes, the desolateness which marked what had but yesterday been the habitations of Korah, Dathan, and Abiram, would only give poignancy to the feeling that with this event a yoke of bondage had been for ever riveted upon the nation. For they recognised not the purpose and meaning of God; this would have implied spiritual discernment; only that, if judgment had proceeded from Jehovah, it had come, if not at the instigation of, yet in order to vindicate Moses and Aaron. In their ingratitude they even forgot that, but for the intercession of these two, the whole congregation would have perished in the gainsaying of Korah. So truly did that generation prove the justice of the Divine sentence that none of their number should enter into the land of Canaan, and so entirely unfit did their conduct (as of old that of Esau) show them for inheriting the promises!

But as for Moses and Aaron, when the congregation was once more gathered against them with this cruel and unjust charge on their lips, "Ye have killed the people of Jehovah," they almost instinctively "faced towards the tent of meeting," [29] as the place whence their help came and to which their appeal was now made. Nor did they look in vain. Denser and more closely than before did the cloud cover the tabernacle, and from out of it burst visibly the luminous glory of Jehovah. And as Moses and Aaron entered the court of the tabernacle, "Jehovah spake. unto Moses, saying. Get you up from among this congregation, and I will consume them as in a moment. And they fell upon their faces." But what was Moses to plead? He knew that "already" was "wrath gone forth from Jehovah," and "the plague" had "begun." What could he now say? In the rebellion at Mount Horeb, [30] again at Kadesh, [31] and but the day before at the gainsaying of Korah, he had exhausted every argument. No similar plea, nor indeed any plea, remained. Then it was, in the hour of deepest need, when every argument that even faith could suggest had been taken away, and Israel was, so to speak, *lost,* that the all-sufficiency of the Divine provision in its vicarious and mediatorial character appeared. Although as yet only *typical,* it proved all sufficient. The incense kindled on the coals taken from the altar of burnt-offering, where the sacrifices had been brought, typified the accepted mediatorial intercession of our great High-priest. And now, when there was absolutely no plea upon earth, this typical pleading of His perfect righteousness and intercession prevailed. Never before or after was the gospel so preached under the Old Testament [32] as when Aaron, at Moses' direction, took the censer, and, having filled it from the altar, "ran into the midst of the congregation," "and put on incense, and made an atonement for the people" (xvi. 47). And as he stood with that censer "between the dead and the living," "the plague," which had already swept away not less than 14,700 men, "was stayed." Thus if Korah's assumption of the priestly functions had caused, the exercise of the typical priesthood now removed, the plague.

But the truth which God now taught the people was not to be exhibited only in judgment. After the storm and the earthquake came the "still, small voice," and the typical import of the Aaronic priesthood was presented under a beautiful symbol. By direction of God, "a rod" for each of the twelve tribes, bearing the respective names of their princes, [33] was laid up in the Most Holy Place, before the Ark of the Covenant. And on the morrow, when Moses entered the sanctuary, "behold the rod of Aaron for the house of Levi had budded, and brought forth buds, and bloomed blossoms, and yielded almonds." The symbolical teaching of this was plain. Each of these "rods" was a ruler's staff, the emblem of a tribe and its government. This was the natural position of all these princes of Israel. But theirs as well as Aaron's were rods *cut off from the parent-stem,* and therefore incapable of putting forth verdure, bearing blossom, or yielding fruit in the sanctuary of God. By nature, then, there was absolutely no difference between Aaron and the other princes; all were equally incapable of the new life of fruitfulness. What distinguished Aaron's rod was the selection of God and the miraculous gift bestowed upon it. And then, typically in the old, but really in the new dispensation, that rod burst at the same time into branches, into blossom, and even into fruit — all these three combined, and all appearing at the same time. And so these princes "took every man his rod;" but Aaron's rod was again brought before the Ark of the Covenant, and kept there "for a token." [34] Nor was even the choice of the almond, which blossoms first of trees, without its deep meaning. For the almond, which bursts earliest into flower and fruit, is called in Hebrew "*the waker*" (*shaked,* comp. Jer. i. 11, 12). Thus, as the "early waker," the Aaronic priesthood, with its buds, blossoms, and fruit, was typical of the better priesthood, when the Sun of Righteousness would rise "with healing in His wings." [35]

[1] Deut. i. 46.

[2] Deut. ii. 1.

[3] Numb. xxxiii. 36.

[4] Gen. xiv, 7.

[5] Or "wandering," or "being shaken." Bishop Harold Browne suggests the query whether there may be any allusion to this in Ps. xxix. 8; "The Lord shaketh the wilderness of Kadesh."

[6] In Deut. x. 6, 7, *four* of these stations are again mentioned, but in the inverse order from Numb. xxxiii. Evidently in Numb. xxxiii. we have the camps from Kadesh to Ezion-gaber during the thirty-seven years of wandering; while in Deut. x. 6, 7 the reference is to the march from Kadesh to Mount Hor in the fortieth year (after the *second* stay at Kadesh) on the journey of Israel to take possession of the land. But the apparently strange insertion of verses 6 and 7 in Deut. x., interrupting a quite different narrative, requires explanation. In vers. 1-5 Moses reminds the people how, in answer to his prayer, God had restored His covenant. Verses 6 and 7 are then inserted to show that not only the covenant, but also the mediatorial office of the high-priesthood had been similarly granted anew. God had not only continued it to Aaron, but, on his death at Mosera, Eleazar had been invested with the office, and under his ministry the tribes had continued their onward march. Instead of explaining all this in detail, Moses simply reminds the children of Israel (vers. 6, 7) of the historical facts of the case, which would speak for themselves.

[7] Gen. xxxvi. 27; 1 Chron. i. 42.

[8] Many of these stations have been identified — at least, with a great degree of probability. But an account of the various suggestions of modern explorers would lead too much into details.

[9] See *Speaker's Commentary,* vol. ii. p. 720, *note.* The clearest indication of this is found in Isa. xliii. 16-21. But I think it a mistake to trace in Ps. lxxiv. 14, an allusion to a supply of fish from the Elanitic Gulf of the Red Sea, although it is true that several of the encampments of Israel were on, or quite close to, its shores.

[10] Numb. xv. 32-36.

[11] Ex. xxxi. 14, etc.; xxxv. 2.

[12] Numb. xvi.

[13] Numb. xvi. 41-50.

[14] Ex. vi. 18.

[15] The statement that Zelophehad, a Manassite, had not been "in the company of Korah" (Numb. xxvii. 3), implies that his fellow-conspirators belonged to the various tribes.

[16] The Authorised Version (Numb. xvi. 2) translates "famous," but the literal rendering is "called to the meeting," evidently members of the national representative council. See Numb. i. 16.

[17] Numb. iii. 27.

[18] We have rendered the term literally by "convocation." Two different terms are used in this chapter. One of these — *edah* — means, literally, *congregation,* and may be said to designate Israel as the outward and visible Church. The other term is *kahal,* literally "the called," or convocation, and refers to the spiritual character of Israel as called of God. Thus the distinction of an outward and visible and a spiritual Church had its equivalent in the Old Testament. In this chapter the term *kahal* occurs only in ver. 3, and again in ver. 33.

[19] From Numb. xvi., and the reference in Numb. xxvi. 10, 11, I am led to infer that Korah followed also in the train, perhaps to see what would come of it, leaving the two hundred and fifty princes at the door of the Tabernacle. If Korah's tent was contiguous to those of Dathan and Abiram, we can form a clearer conception of the whole scene.

[20] Literally rendering xvi. 14: "Wilt thou put out the eyes of these men?"

[21] Jer. xxxi. 30; Ezek. xviii. 19, 20.

[22] Numb. xxvi. 11.

[23] I Sam, i. 1; I Chron. vi. 33-38.

[24] Wrongly translated in the Authorised Version, "for the sons of Korah,"

[25] The following are the eleven Psalms designated as those of the sons of Korah: Ps, xlii., xliv.-xlix., lxxxiv., lxxxv,, lxxxvii,, and lxxxviii. The following are further references to the history of the sons of Korah: I Chron. ix, 19; xii.

6; xxvi, 1-19; 2 Chron, xx. 19; Neh. xi, 19.

[26] Lev. x. 2.

[27] Numb. xvi. 37.

[28] Ps. iv. 4.

[29] This is the literal rendering.

[30] Ex. xxxii. 31.

[31] Numb. xiv. 13, etc.

[32] The only similar instance was the lifting up of the brazen serpent, which typically represented another part of the work of our Redeemer. Even the prophecies of Isaiah were not clearer than these two sermons by outward deed, as we may call them — the one declaring the typical meaning of the Aaronic priesthood, and the efficacy of that to which it pointed; the other, the character and the completeness of God's provision for the removal of guilt.

[33] According to the more common view, twelve rods were presented, Ephraim and Manasseh being counted only one tribe, that of Joseph. According to others, there were twelve rods, exclusively of that of Levi, which bore the name of Aaron.

[34] Apparently, both the pot of manna and Aaron's rod were lost when the ark returned from the Philistine cities (see I Kings viii. 9). This loss also was deeply significant — as it were, God's unspoken comment on the state of Israel.

[35] The significance of the Levitical sections, as they follow upon Numb. xvii., will be apparent to the attentive reader. But this is not the place to enter further on the subject.

Chapter Twenty

(Numb. xx.; xxi. 1-3.)

It was indeed most fitting that, at the end of the thirty-seven years' wanderings, Israel should once more gather at Kadesh. There they had been scattered, when the evil report which the spies had brought led to their unbelief and rebellion; and thence had the old generation carried, as it were, its sentence of death back into the wilderness, till during these long and weary years its full terms had been exhausted. And now a new generation was once more at Kadesh. From the very spot where the old was broken off was the fresh start to be made. God is faithful to His purpose; *He* never breaks off. If the old was interrupted, it had been by man's unbelief and rebellion, not by failure on the part of God; and when He resumed His work, it was exactly where it had been so broken off. And man also must return to where he has departed from God, and to where sentence has been pronounced against him, before he enters on his new journey to the Land of Promise. But what solemn thoughts might not have been expected in this new generation, as they once more stood ready to resume their journeying on the spot where that of their fathers had been arrested. As *He* had sanctified His Name in Kadesh by judgment, would *they* now sanctify it by their faith and willing obedience?

Besides Joshua and Caleb, to whom entrance into the land had been specially promised, only three of the old generation still remained. These were Miriam, Moses, and Aaron. And now, just at the commencement of this fresh start, as if the more solemnly to remind them of the past, Miriam, who had led the hymn of thanksgiving and triumph on their first entering the desert, [1] was taken away. Only Moses and Aaron were now left — weary, wayworn pilgrims, to begin a new journey with new pilgrims, who had to learn afresh the dealings of Jehovah. And this may help us to understand what happened at the very outset of their pilgrimage. Israel was in Kadesh, or rather in the desert of Zin, the name Kadesh applying probably to the whole district as well as to a special locality. So large a number of people gathered in one place would naturally soon suffer from want of water. Let it also be remembered, that that generation knew of the wonders of the Lord chiefly by the hearing of the ear, but of His judgments by what they had seen of death sweeping away all who had come out of Egypt. In the hardness of their hearts it now seemed to them as if the prospect before them were hopeless, and they destined to suffer the same fate as their fathers. Something of this unbelieving despair appears in their cry: "Would God that we had died when our brethren died before Jehovah" [2] — that is, by Divine judgment, during these years of wandering. The remembrance of the past with its disappointments seems to find expression in their complaints (xx. 5). It is as if they contrasted the stay of their nation in Egypt, and the hopes awakened on leaving it, with the disappointment of seeing the good land almost within their grasp, and then being turned back to die in the wilderness! And so the people broke forth in rebellion against Moses and against Aaron.

Feelings similar to theirs seem to have taken hold even on Moses and Aaron — only in a different direction. The people despaired of success, and rebelled against Moses and Aaron. With them as leaders they would never get possession of the Land of Promise. On the other hand, Moses and Aaron also despaired of success, and rebelled, as it were, against the people. Such an unbelieving people, rebelling at the very outset, would never be allowed to enter the land. The people felt as if the prospect before them were hopeless, and so did Moses and Aaron, although on opposite grounds. As we have said, the people rebelled against Moses and Aaron, and Moses and Aaron against the people. But at bottom, the ground of despair and of rebellion, both on the part of the people and of Moses, was precisely the same. In both cases it was really unbelief of God. The people had looked upon Moses and not upon God as their leader into the land, and they had despaired. Moses looked at the people as they were in themselves, instead of thinking of God Who now sent them forward, secure in His promise, which He would assuredly fulfil. This soon appeared in the conduct and language of Moses. By Divine direction he was to stand in sight of the people at "the rock before their eyes" with "the rod from before Jehovah" — no doubt the same with which the miracles had been wrought in Egypt, and under whose stroke water had once before sprung from the rock at Rephidim. [3]

It is generally thought that the sin of Moses, in which Aaron shared, consisted in his *striking* the rock — and doing so twice — instead of merely *speaking* to it, "and it shall give forth its water;" and also, in the hasty and improper language which he used on the occasion: "Hear now, ye rebels, must we fetch you water out of this rock?" [4] But it seems difficult to accept this view. On the one hand, we can scarcely imagine that unbelief should have led Moses to strike, rather than to speak to the rock, as if the former would have been more efficacious than the latter. On the other hand, it seems strange that Moses should have been directed to "take the rod," if he were not to have used it, the more so as this had been the Divinely sanctioned mode of proceeding at Rephidim. [5] Lastly, how, in that case, could Aaron have been implicated in the sin of Moses? Of course, the striking the rock *twice* was, as we read in Psalm cvi. 32, 33, evidence that they had "angered" Moses, and that "his spirit was provoked." This also showed itself in his language, which Scripture thus characterises: "he spake unadvisedly with his lips" — or, as the word literally means, "he babbled." [6] Be it observed, that Moses *is not anywhere in Scripture blamed* for striking instead of speaking to the rock, while it is expressly stated that the people "angered him also at the waters of strife, so that it went ill with Moses for their sakes."

The other aspect of the sin of Moses was afterwards expressly stated by the Lord Himself, when He pronounced on Moses and Aaron the sentence that they should not "bring this congregation into the land," which He had given them, on this ground: "Because ye believed Me not, to sanctify Me in the eyes of the children of Israel" (xx. 12). Thus in their rebellion against Moses and Aaron, the people had not believed that Jehovah would bring them into the land which He had given them; while, in their anger at the people, Moses and Aaron had not believed God, to sanctify Him in His power and grace in the eyes of the children of Israel. Israel failed as the people of God; Moses as their mediator. Hitherto Moses had, under every provocation, been faithful as a steward over his charge, and pleaded with God and prevailed, because he believed. Now for the first time Moses failed, as we all fail, through unbelief, looking at the sin of the people, and thence inferring the impossibility of their inheriting the promises, instead of looking at the grace and power of God which made all things possible, and at the certainty of the promise. Unlike Abraham in similar circumstances, "he staggered at the promises." And having through unbelief failed as mediator of the people, his office was to cease, and the conduct of Israel into the land to devolve upon another.

It is only in this sense that we can accept the common statement, that the sin of Moses was *official* rather than *personal*. For these two — office or work, and person — cannot be separated either as regards responsibility or duty. Rather would we think of Moses and Aaron as aged pilgrims, worn with the long way through the wilderness, and footsore with its roughnesses and stones, whose strength momentarily failed when the weary journey was once more resumed, and who in their weariness stumbled at the rock of offence. Yet few events possess deeper pathos than this "babbling" at the waters of Meribah. Its true parallel is found not in the Old but in the New Testament. It is true that, in similar circumstances, Elijah also despaired of Israel, and was directed to "the mount of God," there to learn the same lesson as Moses — before, like him, he was unclothed of his office. But the full counterpart to the temptation of Moses is presented in the history of John the Baptist, when doubting, not the Person but the mode of working of the Messiah, and despairing, from what he saw and heard, of the fulfilment of the promise at that time and among that generation, he sent his disciples on that memorable embassy, just before he also was unclothed of his office. This is not the place to follow the subject further. Suffice it to point out, on the one hand, Moses, Elijah, John the Baptist, and, on the other, Joshua, Elisha, and our blessed Lord, as the types and antitypes presented to us in Scripture.

Before leaving Kadesh, Moses sent messengers to the king of Edom, and also, as we learn from Judges xi. 17, to the king of Moab, [7] whose dominions lay on the north of Edom, asking permission for Israel to pass through their countries. A glance at the map will show that this would have been the most direct route, if Palestine was to be entered from the other side Jordan at Jericho. Certainly it was the easiest route, as it avoided contact with those who held the Negeb, or south country, who thirty-seven years before had met Israel in hostile conflict and signally defeated them. [8] But in vain Moses urged upon Edom the claims of national kinship, Israel's past sufferings in Egypt, and their marvellous deliverance and guidance by The Angel of Jehovah. In vain also did he limit his request to permission to use the ordinary caravan road — "the king's highway" — without straying either to the right or the left, adding the promise of payment for the use of the wells. [9] The children of Esau not only absolutely refused, but hastily gathered an army of observation on their borders. Meantime, while the messengers of Moses had gone on their embassy, the camp of Israel had moved forward to what may be described as "the uttermost of the border" of Edom. A day's journey eastward from Kadesh, through the wide and broad Wády Murreh, suddenly rises a remarkable mountain, quite isolated and prominent, which Canon Williams describes as "singularly formed," and the late Professor Robinson likens to "a lofty citadel." Its present name Moderah preserves the ancient Biblical Moserah, which, from a comparison of Numb. xx. 22-29 with Deut. x. 6, we know to have been only another designation for Mount Hor. In fact, "Mount Hor" or *Hor-ha-Hor* ("mountain, the mountain") just means "the remarkable mountain." This was the natural route for Israel to take, if they hoped to pass through Edom by the king's highway - the present Wády Ghuweir, - which would have led them by way of Moab, easily and straight, to the other side of Jordan. It was natural for them here to halt and await the reply of the king of Edom. For while Moderah lies at the very boundary, but still outside Edom, it is also at the entrance to the various wddies or roads, which thence open east, south, and south-west, so that the children of Israel might thence take any route which circumstances would indicate. Moreover, from the height of Moderah they would be able to observe any hostile movement that might be directed against them, whether from the east by Edom, or from the north and west by the Amalekites and Canaanites. From what has been said, it will be gathered that we regard this as the Mount Hor where Aaron died. [10]

Thus speedily, within a day's journey of the place of his sin, was the Divine sentence upon Aaron executed. There is a solemn grandeur about this narrative, befitting the occasion and in accordance with the locality. In the sight of all the congregation these three, Moses, Aaron, and Eleazar, went up the mount. In his full priestly dress walked Aaron to his burial. He knew it, and so did all in that camp, who now, for the last time, reverently and silently looked upon the venerable figure of him who, these forty years, had ministered unto them in holy things. [11] There was no farewell. In that typical priesthood all depended on the unbroken continuance of the office, not of the person. And hence on that mountain-top Aaron was first unclothed of his priestly robes, and Eleazar, his son, formally invested with them. Thus the priesthood had not for a moment ceased when Aaron died. Then, not as a priest but simply as one of God's Israel, was he "gathered unto his people." But over that which passed between the three on the mount has the hand of God drawn the veil of silence. And so the new priest, Eleazar, came down from the solemn scene on Mount Hor to minister amidst a hushed and awe-stricken congregation. "And when all the congregation saw that Aaron was dead, they mourned for Aaron thirty days, even all the house of Israel."

Serious tidings were now in store for Israel. The messengers returned from Edom bringing absolute refusal to the request of passage through that country. Not only so, but the large army of Edom was assembling on the frontier, close to the camping-ground of Israel. If, according to the Divine command, Edom was not to be attacked, then Israel must rapidly *retreat*. The ordinary route from Mount Hor "to compass the land of Edom," so as to advance northwards, by the east of Edom, would have led Israel straight down by the Wády El-Jeib, and so through the northern part of the Arabah. But this route touched the western boundary of Edom, just where, as we gather from the Scriptural narrative, the army of Edom was *echeloned*. To avoid them, it became therefore necessary, in the first place, to retrace their steps again through part of the Wády Murreh, in order thence to strike in a southeasterly direction through what are now known as "the mountains of the 'Azâzimeh," the ancient dukedom of Teman, or Mount Paran. By this detour Israel would strike the Arabah far south of where the army of Edom awaited them, passing through the modern Wádies Ghudhâghidh and 'Adbeh. In point of fact, we learn from Deut. x. 7 that Gudgodah and Jotbath were the two stations reached next after the retreat from Mount Hor. But just at the point where the host of Israel would turn southwards from Wády Murreh, they were also in almost a straight line for the territory of the king of Arad. Of course, he would be informed that Israel had been refused a passage through Edom, and, finding them on the flank of his territory, would naturally imagine that they intended to invade it. "And the Canaanitish king of Arad, which dwelt in the Negeb" [12] (or south country), "heard tell that Israel came by the way of the spies" (or, more probably, "the way of the merchants," the caravan road); [13] "then he fought against Israel, and took of them prisoners" — having probably fallen on their rearguard. The event is mentioned for this twofold reason: to show the unprovoked enmity of Canaan against Israel, and the faithfulness of God. For Israel at that time "vowed a vow" utterly to destroy the cities of the Canaanites. And God hearkened and heard. Many years afterwards He gave the prayed-for victory, [14] when the name of Hormah or ban — utter destruction — given in prophetic anticipation of God's faithfulness, became a reality. [15]

[1] Ex. xv. 21.

[2] Numb. xx. 3.

[3] Ex. xvii. 6.

[4] The great Rabbinical interpreter Rashi accounts for the twice striking; by supposing that Moses went to the wrong rock, when, at the first stroke, only a few drops came, but at the second abundance of water. Pie finds the sin of Moses in his striking instead of speaking, since the people would, in the latter case, have argued — If the rock which neither speaks, hears, nor needs nourishment, obeys the voice of God, how much more are we bound so to do. The Jerusalem Targum has it, that at the first stroke blood came from the rock.

[5] Ex. xvii. 6.

[6] The word, whether written *bata* or *bada*, means to talk foolishly, or rashly, *to babble*, also to boast.

[7] The reply of the king of Moab is not mentioned in Scripture, because, upon the refusal of Edom, even his permission would have been of no use, as the road to Moab lay through Edom.

[8] Numb. xiv. 44, 45.

[9] Numb. xx. 14-17.

[10] The traditional site for Mount Hor is Jebel Harûn, close by Petra, the capital of Edom. To state is already to re-

fute a supposition which implies that Israel had asked leave to pass through Edom, and then, without awaiting the reply, marched into the heart of Edom, and camped for thirty days close by its capital! Moreover, it is difficult to understand what could have been the object of going so far south, if Israel hoped — as at the time they did — to strike through the nearest practicable wády, the road that led northward through Edom and Moab to the ford of Jordan. In that case Jebel Harûn would have been far out of their way. Finally, it is impossible to arrange the chronological succession of events as given in the Bible, except on the supposition that Moderah was Mount Hor. For, if the camp of Israel had been near Petra, there could have been no reason for the king of Arad to dread their forcing their way through his territory (Numb. xxi. 1), even as it seems most unlikely that he should have marched so far southeast as Petra to attack Israel. Accordingly, interpreters who regard Jebel Harûn as Mount Hor are obliged to suppose that the attack of the king of Arad had taken place earlier, say, at the period indicated in Numb. xx. 22. But in that case it is difficult to imagine how the king could have heard that Israel was "coming by the way of the spies," seeing they were taking exactly the opposite direction, and had just requested permission to pass through Edom. Against these weighty reasons we have only the authority of tradition in favour of Harun, On the other hand, all becomes plain, and easily understood, if we regard Moderah as Mount Hor; and the whole narrative in its chronological succession in Scripture is just what we should have expected. The reader who wishes further information is referred to the admirable work of the late Rev. E. Wilton on *The Negeb, or South Country of Scripture* (pp. 126-134), and to the excellent map attached to it.

[11] According to Numb. xxxiii. 37, etc., Aaron died on the first day of the fifth month of the fortieth year after the Exodus, and at the age of one hundred and twenty-three years.

[12] So literally. Arad is the modern Tell Arad, about twenty miles south of Hebron. So tenaciously do names cling to localities in the East.

[13] So Mr. Wilton rightly renders it, and not "the way of the spies," *i.e.*, of the twelve men who had, thirty-eight years before, gone up to spy the land. Others translate, "the beaten track."

[14] Judges i. 17.

[15] Some commentators imagine that even at the first a great victory had been gained by the Israelites over the Canaanites. But the supposition is incompatible alike with the narrative and with other portions of Scripture.

Chapter Twenty-One

(Numb. xxi. 3-35; xxxiii. 35-49; Deut. ii.-iii. 11.)

The opposition of Edom and the unprovoked attack of the Canaanite king of Arad must have convinced Israel that the most serious difficulties of their march had now commenced. It was quite natural that, during the thirty-eight years when they were scattered up and down in the Sinaitic peninsula, their powerful neighbours should have left them unmolested, as the wandering Bedawin are at this day. [1] But when Israel again gathered together and moved forward as a host, then the tidings of the marvellous things which God had done for them, communicated with all the circumstantiality common in the east, would excite mingled terror and a determination to resist them. The latter probably first; the former as resistance was seen to be vain, and the God of Israel realised as stronger than all other national deities. Eastern idolaters would naturally thus reason; and the knowledge of this will help our understanding of the Scriptural narrative.

The general direction of Israel's march, in order to "compass" the land of Edom, was first to the head of the Elanitic Gulf of the Red Sea, or the Gulf of 'Akabah. Thence they would, a few hours north of Ezion-gaber (the giant's backbone), enter the mountains, and then pass northwards, marching to Moab "by the road which runs between Edom and the limestone plateau of the great eastern desert" [2] (comp. Deut. ii. 8). Probably they were prepared to contend for every fresh advance which they made northwards. But the first part of their journey was otherwise trying. That deep depression of the Arabah through which they marched — intensely hot, bare of vegetation, desolate, rough, and visited by terrible sandstorms — was pre-eminently "that great and terrible wilderness." of which Moses afterwards reminded the people. [3] What with the weariness of the way, the want of water, and of all food other than the manna, "the soul of the people was much discouraged," "and the people spake against God and against Moses." The judgment of "fiery serpents" which the Lord, "in punishment, sent among the people," and of which so many died, bore a marked resemblance to all His former dealings. Once more He did not create a new thing for the execution of His purpose, but only disposed sovereignly of what already existed. Travellers give remarkable confirmation and illustrations of the number and poisonous character of the serpents in that district. [4] Thus one writes of the neighbourhood of the gulf: "The sand on the shore showed traces of snakes on every hand. They had crawled there in various directions. Some of the marks appeared to have been made by animals which could not have been less than two inches in diameter. My guide told me that snakes were very common in these regions." Another traveller on exactly the route of the children of Israel states: "In the afternoon a large and very mottled snake was brought to us, marked with *fiery* spots and spiral lines, which evidently belonged, from the formation of its teeth, to one of the most poisonous species...The Bedouins say that these snakes, of which they have great dread, are very numerous in this locality." [5] From the fact that the brazen serpent is also called "*fiery*" (a *Saraph*), we infer that the expression describes rather the appearance of these "fire-snakes" than the effect of their bite.

Two things are most marked in this history — the speedy repentance of Israel, couched in unwonted language of humility, [6] and the marvellous teaching of the symbol, through which those who had been mortally bitten were granted restoration to life and health. Moses was directed to make a fiery serpent of brass, and to set it upon a pole, and whosoever looked upon it was immediately healed. From the teaching of our Lord [7] we know that this was a direct type of the lifting up of the Son of Man, "that whosoever believeth in Him should not perish, but have eternal life." The *simplicity* of the remedy — only to look up in faith, its *immediateness* and its *completeness,* as well as the fact that this was the only but also the *all-sufficient* remedy for the deadly wound of the serpent — all find their counterpart in the Gospel. But for the proper understanding both of the type and of the words of our Lord, we must inquire in what manner Israel would view and understand the lifting up of the brazen serpent and the healing that flowed from it Undoubtedly, Israel would at once connect this death through the fiery serpents with the introduction of death into Paradise through the serpent. [8] And now a brazen serpent was lifted up, made in the likeness of the fiery serpent, yet *without its poisonous bite.* And this was for the healing of Israel. Clearly then, the deadly poison of the fiery serpent was removed in the uplifted brazen serpent! All this would carry back the mind to the promise given when first the poisonous sting of the serpent was felt, that the Seed of the Woman should bruise the head of the serpent, and that in so doing His own heel should be bruised. In this sense even the apocryphal Book of Wisdom (xvi. 6) designates the brazen serpent "a symbol of salvation." And so we are clearly taught that "God sending His own Son in *the likeness of sinful flesh,* and for sin, *condemned sin in the flesh;*" [9] that "He hath made Him to be sin for us, who knew no sin;" [10] and that "His own self bare our sins in His own body on the tree." [11] The precious meaning of the type is thus deduced by Luther from the three grand peculiarities of this "symbol of salvation:" "First, the serpent which Moses made at the command of God had to be of brass or copper, that is, red, and like those fiery serpents, which were red, and burning in their bite — yet without poison. Secondly, the brazen serpent had to be set up on a pole for a sign" (comp. Col. ii. 14, etc.). "Thirdly, those who would be healed of the fiery serpents' bite must look up to the brazen serpent, lifted up on the pole" (perceive, and believe), "else they could not recover nor live." Similarly a modern German critic thus annotates John iii. 14: "Christ is the antitype of this serpent, inasmuch as He took upon Himself and vicariously bore sin, the most noxious of all noxious powers."

It is of the deepest interest to follow the march of the children of Israel, when every day's journey brought them nearer to the Land of Promise as their goal. To them it was not, as to us, a land of ruins and of memories, but of beauty and of hope. To a people who had all their lives seen and known nothing but "the wilderness," the richness, fertility, and varied beauty of Palestine, as it then was, must have possessed charms such as we can scarcely imagine. Then every step in advance was, so to speak, under the direct leading of God, and, in a sense, a miracle, while every such leading and miracle was itself a pledge of others yet to follow. The researches of modern travellers [12] enable us almost to company with Israel on this their march. As already stated, the wonderful tenacity with which old names keep their hold in the far East helps us to discover the exact spots of Biblical scenes; while, on the other hand, descriptions of the localities throw most vivid light on the Scriptural narratives, and afford evidence of their trustworthiness.

The reader ought to remember that the route which lay before Israel was in part the same as that still traversed by the great caravans from Damascus to Mecca. The territories which they successively passed or entered were occupied as follows. First, Israel skirted along the *eastern* boundary of Edom, leaving it on their left. The *western* boundary of Edom, through which Israel had sought a passage when starting from Kadesh, [13] would from its mountainous character and few passes have been easily defended against the Israelites. But it was otherwise with the eastern line of frontier, which lay open to Israel^ had they not been Divinely directed not to fight against Edom. [14] This, however, explains the friendly attitude which the Edomites found it prudent to adopt along their eastern frontier, [15] although their army had shortly before been prepared to fight on the western. At *Ije Abarim*, [16] "the ruins," or "the hills of the passages," or "of the sides" — perhaps "the lateral hills" — the Israelites were approaching the wilderness which lay to the east of Moab. The brook or Wády Zared [17] here forms the boundary between Edom and Moab. But as Israel had been also commanded not to fight against Moab, [18] they left their territory equally untouched, and, continuing straight northwards, passed through the wilderness of Moab, till they reached the river Arnon, the modern Wady Mojib, which formed the boundary between the Moabites and the Amorites. The territory of the Amorites stretched from the Arnon to the Jabbok. It had originally belonged to the Moabites; [19] but they had been driven southwards by the Amorites. No command of God prevented Israel from warring against the Amorites, and when Sihon, their king, refused to give them a free passage through his territory, they were Divinely directed to that attack which issued in the destruction of Sihon, and the possession of his land by Israel.

At the brook Zared — on the southern boundary of Moab — the Israelites had already been in a line with the Dead Sea, leaving it, of course, far on their left. The river Amon also, which formed the boundary between Moab and the Amorites, flows into the Dead Sea almost opposite to Hazazon-tamar, or En-gedi. This tract, which now bears the name of el-Belkah, is known to the reader of the Old Testament as the *land of Gilead*, while in New Testament times it formed the province of *Perea*. Lastly, the district north of the Jabbok and east of the Jordan was the ancient *Bashan*, or the modern Hauran. The fact that the country north of the Amon had, before its possession by the Amorites, been so long held by Moab explains the name "Fields of Moab" (rendered in the Authorised Version "country of Moab," Numbers xxi. 20) as applied to the upland hills of Gilead, just as the western side of Jordan similarly bore the name of "the plains of Moab," or rather "the lowlands of Moab." [20] The children of Israel were still camped on the *south* side of the Amon when they sent the embassy to Sihon, demanding a passage through his territory. Canon Tristram has given a most vivid description of the rift through which the Amon flows. Its width is calculated at about three miles from crest to crest, and its depth at 2150 feet from the top of the southern, and at 1950 from that of the northern bank. Of course, the army of Israel could not have passed the river here, but higher up, to the east, "in the wilderness." [21] They probably waited till the messengers returned from Sihon. How high their courage and confidence in God had risen, when tidings arrived that Sihon with all his army was coming to meet them, appears even from those extracts of poetic pieces which form so marked a peculiarity of the Book of Numbers, and which read like stanzas of war-songs by the camp-fires. [22] From the banks of the Amon the route of Israel was no doubt northward till they reached Bainoth or Bamoth Baal, "the heights of Baal," [23] one of the stations afterwards taken up by Balak and Balaam. [24] "And from Bamoth (they marched) to the valley, which is in the fields of Moab (on the plateau of Moab), on the height of Pisgah, and looks over to the face of the wilderness," [25] that is, over the tract of land which extends to the north-eastern shore of the Dead Sea. [26]

From this plateau on the mountains of the Abarim, of which Pisgah and Nebo were peaks, Israel had its first view of the Land of Promise, and especially of that mysterious Sea of Salt whose glittering surface and deathlike surroundings would recall such solemn memories and warnings. At last then the goal was in view! The decisive battle between Sihon and Israel was fought almost within sight of the Dead Sea. The victory at Jahaz, in which Sihon was smitten "with the edge of the sword" — that is, without quarter or sparing, — gave Israel possession of the whole country, including Heshbon and "all the daughters thereof" — or daughter-towns, — from the Arnon to the upper Jabbok (the modern Nahr Amman). The latter river formed the boundary between the Amorites and the Ammonites. Beyond this the Amorites had not penetrated, because "the border of the children of Ammon was strong." [27] And Israel also forbore to penetrate farther, not on the same ground as the Amorites, but because of an express command of God. [28] Leaving untouched therefore the country of Ammon, the Israelites next moved northward, defeated Og, king of Bashan, and took possession of his territory also, and of the mountains of Gilead. [29] The whole country east of the Jordan was now Israel's, and the passage of that river could not be disputed.

Before actually entering upon their long-promised inheritance, some great lessons had, indeed, yet to be learned. An event would take place which would for ever mark the relation between the kingdom of God and that of this world. The mission of Moses, the servant of the Lord, must also come to an end, and the needful arrangements be made for possessing and holding the land of Palestine. But all these belong, strictly speaking, to another period of Israel's history. When the camp was pitched in *Shittim*, "on this side Jordan by Jericho," waiting for the signal to cross the boundary-line, *the wanderings of the children of Israel* were really at an end.

[1] This is well brought out in Palmer's *Desert of the Exodus,* Part ii., pp. 517, etc.

[2] *Desert of the Exodus,* vol. ii. p. 523.

[3] Deut. i. 19.

[4] For many and very apt Scripture illustrations we would here refer to Mr. Wilton's *Negeb*, p. 47, etc.

[5] Kurtz' *History of the Old Covenant*, vol. iii. pp. 343, 344, English translation.

[6] Numb. xxi. 7.

[7] John iii. 14, 15.

[8] Both the Jerusalem and the Jonathan Targum contain an allusion to this.

[9] Rom. viii. 3.

[10] 2 Cor. v. 21.

[11] 1 Pet. ii. 24.

[12] We cannot, of course, here enter on a description of these localities as illustrative of the Bible, however interesting the subject. For further information we direct the reader, besides the works of Professor Robinson, Canon Williams, Mr. Wilton, and Professor Palmer, to Canon Tristram's *Land of Moab*, as specially illustrative of this part of our history.

[13] Numb. xx. 18.

[14] Deut. ii. 4-6.

[15] Deut. ii. 29.

[16] There is reason to suppose that *Abarim,* or "passages," was a generic name for the mountains which bordered the territory of Moab.

[17] Numb. xxi. 12.

[18] Deut. ii. 9.

[19] Numb. xxi. 26.

[20] Numb. xxii. 1.

[21] Numb. xxi. 13.

[22] Not less than three of these "songs" are quoted in Numb. xxi. We cannot here refer further to these deeply interesting compositions. Similarly, it is impossible to enter into fuller geographical details, or to compare the list of stations in Numb. xxi. with that in chap. xxxiii. and in Deut. ii. But the most perfect harmony prevails between them.

[23] Numb. xxi. 19.

[24] Numb. xxii. 41.

[25] So literally.

[26] Numb. xxi. 20.

[27] Numb. xxi. 24.

[28] Deut. ii. 19.

[29] These territories and their ancient sites have of late been visited and described by such travellers as Canon Tristram, Professor Palmer, and others.